GOOD
FOOD
FOR MEN

Gabriel Gaté's

GOOD FOOD FOR MEN

Photography by John Hay

NEW HOLLAND

First published in 1998 by
New Holland Publishers (UK) Ltd
London • Cape Town • Sydney • Singapore

24 Nutford Place
London W1H 6DQ
United Kingdom

80 McKenzie Street
Cape Town 8001
South Africa

3/2 Aquatic Drive
Frenchs Forest, NSW 2086
Australia

ISBN 1 85974 043 X

Edited by Molly Perham
Designed and illustrated by Luisa Laino
Food styling by Gabriel Gaté and John Hay

Reproduction by
Dot Gradation, UK
Printed and bound in Singapore by
Kyodo Printing Co (Singapore) Pte Ltd

10 9 8 7 6 5 4 3 2 1

Foreword

Welcome to Gabriel Gaté's *Good Food for Men*. This is the book that should prove once and for all that healthy food need not simply be endured, but can be enjoyed. If your notion of nutrition is brown rice and cabbage, think again. This book has a mouth-watering selection of meals that include everything from stir-fried chicken to fresh fruit platters. The fact that you are reading this shows that you have an interest in tasty dishes that act as a nutritionally protective shield to assist you in the fight against cancer.

There is, after all, nothing quite as satisfying as a good meal. After a day at work, I always look forward to having a tasty dish which revives and revitalizes me. We are all faced with a number of food choices – some good, some not so good, and it is easy to make the wrong decisions. The pull of a convenience meal can sometimes seem more alluring than an evening spent slumped over a hot stove – especially if you have had a hard day. Certainly the pace of today's modern lifestyle seems to afford little opportunity of creating a well-balanced meal. But with a bit of planning and a little thought, you can create hundreds of dishes which look good, taste good and do your body the power of good.

The recipe for a healthy diet is to eat roughly five portions of fruit and vegetables (fresh or frozen) a day, include plenty of high-fibre cereals and limit your intake of fat. Evidence shows that people whose diets are rich in cereal fibre have a lower risk of developing bowel cancer. Immediately, you will feel fitter and, more importantly, you will be helping to reduce your risk of developing stomach and bowel cancer.

I feel it is vitally important that we all eat sensibly, which is one of the main reasons why I was delighted to be asked to write this foreword. The food you consume today will help to provide the protection you need for a healthy future. I predict that *Good Food for Men* will soon become a welcome addition to any kitchen because, like the meals featured, it provides a mix of simplicity and nutrition and it is all done with impeccable good taste.

Professor Gordon McVie

Director General, Cancer Research Campaign

Acknowledgments

Most of all I would like to thank my wife, Angie, for her support and assistance in writing this book. I am grateful for the endorsement given to the book by the Cancer Research Campaign and wish to thank its Director General, Professor Gordon McVie. It was a joy to work with Adrian Collette and his team at Reed Books. Thanks go to Sue Hines, the driving force behind the book, and to John Hay, Kirsten Alexander, Foong Ling Kong, Luisa Laino, Julie Pinkham and Rod Howard. Thanks also to my sons, Sebastian and Michael, and to the many friends who helped in various ways, especially Janet Wang for her advice on Asian food, Terry Greguol and Mario Russo from Mario's greengrocer, Henrique Godinho of Casa Portuguesa, Jonathan Gianfreda of Jonathan's of Collingwood, Gianni Omizzolo from Donnini's Pasta, Kusum-Chhotu of Bombay Bazaar, all at Claringbold's Fish Shop and to many others at the Prahran Market. My grateful thanks to our staff at the Gabriel Gaté Cookware Shop in Hawthorn, in particular Robyn Campbell-Wood. Lastly, thanks to all the men who helped by answering my questionnaire.

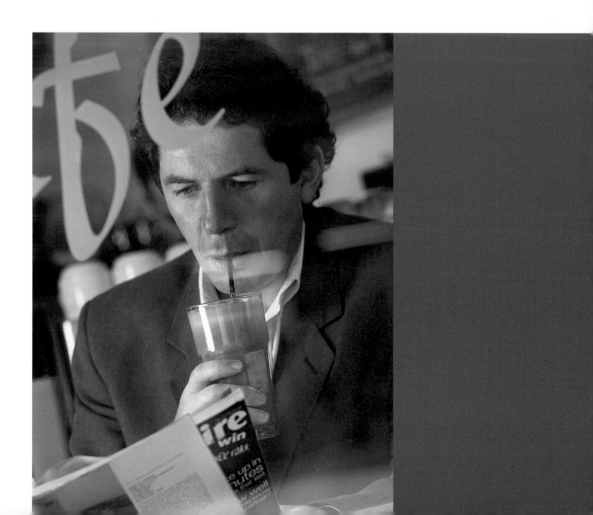

What this Book will do for You

When I first started work on *Good Food for Men* I was encouraged by the interest my project aroused among my male and female friends. The title itself stimulated much discussion and the questions most often asked were 'What's the difference between food for men and food for women?' and 'Isn't the title a little bit sexist?'.

Not being able to cook has been a problem for too many men and women for too long. In all my time cooking and teaching I have also observed that, generally, men don't have as good a knowledge as women when it comes to food, just as boys are not encouraged to contribute to the family cooking the way girls are. Men love to eat, but they do less food shopping and cooking than women. In my own cooking classes, which are open to both sexes, there is, on average, one man for every ten women. Ultimately the choices men make in regard to food, health and independence are affected by this lack of culinary experience and knowledge.

Good Food for Men will serve many functions. The first and most important is that it be used by both men and women as a guide to cooking and eating for well-being. The second, and closer to my heart, is that it will encourage men to cook for themselves for pleasure and independence. The third is that it can help both men and women become better cooks. Cooking is a wonderful skill and being able to cook is a source of great sensual pleasure, a social asset, and a splendid way to boost self-esteem.

I urge you to read the sections on Cooking and Eating for Well-being (p. 28) and How to Become a Good Cook (p. 2) before you start. By the time you have read them you will have already become a better cook.

If you love delicious food, wish to enjoy long-lasting health and possess a secret desire to become a good cook, and if you want to know what food is best for all members of your family, then this book is for you.

Best wishes, and happy cooking!
Gabriel Gaté

CON

tents

introd

uction

HOW to become A Good COOK

The skills of good cooking can be learnt by anybody, and as with most skills, the younger you learn the easier it is. However, the task of learning as an adult can be made easier if you draw on your past experience, observations and cultural background. You will progress more quickly if you cook regularly and practise new dishes that introduce you to new foods, new seasonings and new techniques, and you will be further encouraged if you buy the best fresh foods you can afford. Try not to become disheartened by occasional failures – you can learn as much from them as from your successes. And you will have many successes. Cooking is one of the only crafts in which even a novice can create something marvellous! Share your knowledge and learn from more experienced cooks around you.

Encourage your teenage children to cook and share your knowledge with them.

MEMORISE YOUR EXPERIENCE

Memory is a most important asset in cooking. It is the guardian of our experience. While shopping, try to take in all aspects of as many foods as you can. An acute and well-trained sense of smell and taste, for instance, will help you ascertain the freshness of meat, fish and vegetables.

Smelling

Smelling plant foods must be one of the greatest pleasures we can indulge in. Think of the wonderful aromas of basil, mango, ginger, peach, cumin, rosemary, mandarin, lavender, lemon and coffee. When you smell a peach, for example, your experience will tell you if the peach is at its best or not. If that peach is the best one you have ever smelt, that smell will take the place of honour in your memory cells and become the model. Try recording the smells of certain liquids, such as oils (walnut, olive, corn), vinegars, wines, liqueurs, bottled sauces and so on. The more you allow your sense of smell to develop, the easier it is to differentiate between good and mediocre food. When you cook, the aromas coming from your pots, pans and oven also carry messages. An experienced cook will be able to interpret those messages perfectly. For example, an Italian cook can smell when the bolognese sauce is cooked; a baker can tell when the bread is ready to come out of the oven just by smelling it.

Touching

You also need to develop a very subtle sense of touch to become a good cook. Cooking is a gentle craft, and it is always a great spectacle to watch a good cook choose, prepare, and cook fresh ingredients. With experience, your sense of touch will help you select food and assess its texture, maturity and ripeness. At every stage your hands play a major role in the process of food preparation, so do not be afraid to use them; it would certainly be difficult to choose an avocado without touching it. Your hands also perform the manual cooking tasks like slicing, cutting and chopping, so practise using kitchen implements such as a knife properly, and try to master new cutting techniques. Practice will also help you get a feel for the ingredients.

Looking

Our sense of sight plays an invaluable part in every aspect of food preparation, especially during the cooking process, in anticipating the changes that occur to food as it cooks. We often underestimate the knowledge that we gain from focusing on our cooking or from watching others cook. I assure you that these accumulated experiences will make you a better cook.

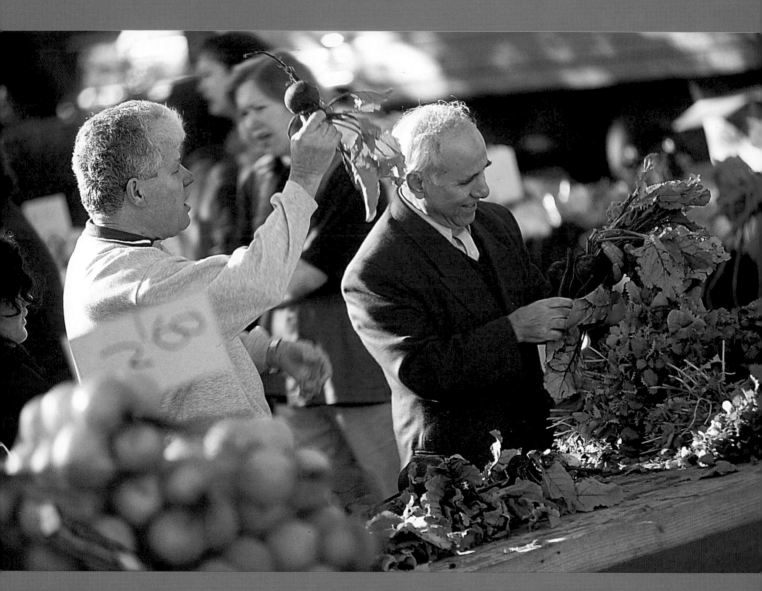

Focus carefully on what you buy.
Teach yourself to choose the best
and freshest produce.

Tasting and Texture

Likewise, take every opportunity to taste food, especially new foods, and smell foods when they are in season (and therefore at their best) to refresh your memory. When tasting, think of the flavours. Is it sweet, salty, sour, acidic or a mixture?

And what of the textures? Our lips, mouth and tongue are extremely sensitive and thrill at the various components in a dish. In some dishes the texture of the ingredients is as important as the taste.

Think of the softness of ice-cream, or the hot potato chip, which is crisp on the outside and soft on the inside. Think of a mixed salad of crisp leaves, crunchy nuts, melt-in-the-mouth avocado and an oily, slippery dressing. You'll be surprised how your cooking can improve when you pay attention to contrasting textures as well as flavour.

Texture can be controlled in several ways. One is in the ingredients you choose. Certain ingredients simply need to be cut in a different style to offer a different texture. Think of the difference between grated carrot and small carrot sticks, between finely shredded lettuce and whole leaves. Cooking methods or techniques also control texture. To my taste, for example, a carrot purée served with a grilled steak is more exciting than steamed whole carrots. Look at some of the photographs in this book and consider the ways in which the various textures of the ingredients contribute to the enjoyment of a dish. Next time you visit your favourite restaurant, take note of all the little things the chef has added to stimulate your senses and palate – it may be the egg, nuts, herbs, vegetables cut in different ways, olives, seeds or fruit.

When you like a particular preparation, try to find out its ingredients and memorize them if possible. The memory of a wide range of tastes and textures will give you the same freedom in your cooking that a musician has when playing without the written music.

COOKING WITH BOTH SIDES OF THE BRAIN

It is now recognized by experts that the right and left sides of the brain have different functions. The right side of the brain is associated with imagination, artistry, music and creativity, while the left side is linked to logic, planning and organization.

Applied to the kitchen this means that the right side of the brain is the creative cook while the left side is the efficient organizer and cleaner. So when preparing a meal, those who use only the right side of their brain usually prepare beautiful food but leave behind a big mess (and get into trouble with the people they live with!). Others who overwork the left side of their brain have a spotless kitchen but the cooking is usually not too great, for they focus more on the cleaning up than the cooking.

Do you recognize yourself somewhere here? The lucky ones are those whose right and left sides of the brain complement one another. Experts on the subject of brain power tend to agree that it would be best to allow each side of the brain to take turns, as the two sides don't seem to work well at the same time – it is a bit like two people speaking simultaneously.

When you want to be creative while cooking, stopping every two minutes to clean can cause the creative flow to disappear and you lose interest. From my experience, people who do not really enjoy cooking are affected by the left side of their brain, which overpowers the right. Experienced writers know that one cannot write creatively (right brain) and edit (left brain) at the same time. The improvement and editing come *after* the writing.

In the preparation of meals the process is similar. Once you have planned what to cook and have bought your ingredients, the left side of the brain gets into gear. You tidy up your workbench and read your recipe carefully; you prepare your equipment; sort out the ingredients and do the peeling and cleaning jobs. Then, when all of the preparation is done and the ingredients are assembled, the left side of the brain can rest and allow the right side to focus on the wonderful task of making the dish.

So don't let the left side nag you while you concentrate. Get rid of distractions such as the television, phone calls and heavy discussions. Let your mind be with the dish, otherwise the pleasures of cooking will be diminished. After you have enjoyed your meal, let the left side of the brain get back to work to look after the cleaning. And when several people live together it is a bonus if everyone shares the cleaning tasks.

Next time you prepare a meal, try to become more aware of when the left and right sides of your brain are functioning. It is quite fun, really.

LEARNING to COOK A NEW DISH

Whether you are a novice or experienced cook, the easiest way to become a better cook is to learn new dishes. Cooking a new dish introduces you to new ingredients, new seasonings, new techniques, and, sometimes, new cookware. As you become more confident and experienced, move on to more challenging or involved recipes. When you start learning choose a simple dish to cook, such as a soup, salad, pasta or fruit salad. And remember that even when cooking for others, it is best to prepare a dish you would enjoy eating yourself; it is difficult to become enthusiastic about cooking something you dislike.

In this book you will find many simple dishes to try. You can also try your hand at familiar dishes you like, such as those your parents or friends have cooked for you in the past. I highly recommend selecting something you have either seen demonstrated on television or featured in a magazine or cookbook. Having prior knowledge about the dish gives you more confidence and direction, whereas attempting a recipe you know nothing about is a bit like walking in the dark. Avoid cooking more than one new dish at a time. Take it slowly, for a new experience can be mentally and physically trying.

Once you have the written recipe in hand, read it all the way through carefully to work out a few things. First, are the ingredients available and in season? You can't get figs in spring but you might be able to substitute cherries or the first of the stone fruits. A certain type of fish or vegetable in a recipe can be easily substituted for another, according to the season. Make sure you have the necessary equipment and try to understand and work through the various steps of the recipe.

Try the following mental exercise:

Imagine breaking 3 eggs into a medium-sized glass bowl. Season with a small pinch of salt, a little freshly ground black pepper and 1 tablespoon chopped parsley. Using a hand whisk, mix in 250 ml (9 fl oz) milk, whisking for 10 seconds until the mixture is runny.

For a change, prepare a pasta dish you've never tried before.

Performing this exercise will help you understand how important it is to concentrate when you read a recipe. By the time you have finished reading, you ought to have an idea of the steps involved and approximately how long it will take to prepare the dish. Remember that the time indicated in a recipe is only a guide, and that it almost always takes longer on the first try.

Carefully choose the day you intend to cook your dish, and take into consideration the time required for the shopping, the preparation and the cooking. Avoid days when you may be tired, rushed or distracted. In this way, you can plan for the experience to be a pleasant one.

Prepare a detailed shopping list (p. 12) and check your pantry, refrigerator or freezer to see which ingredients and seasonings you already have, checking their use-by dates as well. Organize the order in which to do your shopping. First buy the least perishable foods, such as potatoes and pumpkin, followed by more perishable items, such as fish and dairy foods. When shopping on a hot day, try to park your car in the shade and avoid leaving delicate ingredients in a hot car for too long. If the weather is very hot, it is a good idea to have a coolbox in the boot.

Just before beginning to cook, read the whole recipe through carefully. Avoid rushing, and try to concentrate calmly on the task. Your first attempt at a dish may be a great success and, whether pleased or not with the result, you will have learnt a lot and be on the way to becoming a better cook. While cooking, take notes – perhaps the pan got too hot during cooking or the cake took another 10 minutes in your oven – they will be of great help to you the next time you try the dish.

I can't stress enough how important it is to cook the same dish at least once or twice again soon after, in order to build on what you have learnt and to memorize the experience. There have been many times when I have been not quite satisfied with my first attempt, but I only feel that I fail if I give up then. The second time around is so much easier, and by the third the experience is a pleasure. You will see that practice makes a huge difference.

Imagine how much better a cook you can become if you give yourself the easy task of learning a new dish or two a month. Mark off the days in your diary when you will cook your next three or four new dishes and write the names of the recipes in the calendar.

The Art of Having Everything Ready at the Same Time

In cooking, as in music, timing is all important. You want all the elements of a meal (vegetables, fish or meat, pasta, rice, potatoes) to be ready at about the same time. Before starting to cook, take time to think. Quickly rehearse in your mind the various steps in the preparation and establish the order of doing things. Sometimes a recipe may suggest a particular order that does not suit you because you lack the ideal equipment, so you may need to reconsider how you will go about it.

Remember that you can keep many foods warm for a little while in a very low oven at 110°C/225°F/Gas Mark ¼. Just cover the food with foil to stop it from drying out. Vegetables can be kept warm in a steamer with the heat turned off and the lid on, and foods can be reheated briefly in the microwave. When you cook a dish of pan-fried or grilled meat or fish with vegetables, start cooking the vegetables first so as to have them ready just before the meat or fish. When cooking a large roast, such as a leg of lamb, begin by cooking the meat first, followed by the roast vegetables, and lastly, the greens. For a small roast that takes less than 30 minutes, start by roasting the vegetables first.

For pasta dishes, make sure the sauce is made before you put on the pasta. For stir-fry dishes, do all the cutting before starting to cook, and in most cases, stir-fry the vegetables separately before the meat. When noodles are served with a stir-fry dish, cook them first and then mix with the vegetables and meat. When serving a salad with a quick meal, prepare the salad leaves and dressing first; toss them together only at the last minute.

Most casserole dishes and soups can be prepared several hours, or even a day or two, in advance. They will taste better, too, if the flavours are allowed to mature. Avoid leaving the cooking of such dishes until the last moment as they can take longer than anticipated.

Most vegetables take between 8 and 15 minutes to cook if you are steaming, and a little less if boiling. Dry pasta takes 9 to 12 minutes to cook; fresh pasta requires less time. White rice needs about 17 to 20 minutes, while brown rice takes 35 to 40 minutes. Pan-fried or grilled steak takes 5 to 10 minutes. A pan-fried chicken fillet takes between 8 and 15 minutes. A roasted leg of lamb takes 45 minutes to 1 hour in an oven at 180°F/350°F/Gas Mark 4. A medium roast chicken takes 45 minutes to 1 hour at 180°C/350°F/Gas Mark 4. oven. Roast beef takes about 35 minutes per kilogram (2 lb 4 oz) at 180°C/350°F/Gas Mark 4. In the same oven a chicken casserole takes 30 to 40 minutes, while a beef casserole needs 1 to 2 hours. When you cook for a large number, ask for help in serving the food. That way everyone will be able to enjoy and share in the meal.

Discover the Magic of Herbs and Spices

The intensity of flavour in herbs and spices can change a rather bland dish into a masterpiece in seconds. Supermarkets these days offer a choice of dozens of spices, and any good greengrocer will have at least half a dozen varieties of fresh herbs all year round. To become familiar with herbs and spices, use them one at a time in your cooking so you can learn, and memorize, their flavours. For example, start by adding a little sliced basil to pasta or over some sliced tomato, or by using ginger in your next stir-fry. Once you know the individual flavours, and which goes best with what, you can then blend them. Most traditional ethnic foods have the distinctive flavours of certain herbs, spices and seasonings – try to see if you can taste them the next time you visit a restaurant or try out a new dish.

Following are some of the flavours you might encounter:

Greece	Olive oil, lemon, oregano
Italy, France	Olive oil, garlic, basil or parsley
South of France	Olive oil, thyme, tomato, garlic
Hungary	Onion, paprika
Mexico	Tomato, chilli
Spain	Olive oil, onion, tomato, saffron
North Africa	Tomato, cumin, chilli, coriander, cinnamon, olive oil
India	Onion, garlic, ginger, curry spice mix
Thailand	Fish sauce, spices, chilli, lemongrass, coriander
China	Ginger, garlic, soy sauce, rice wine

It is a common belief that the more spices or herbs used in a dish, the better it will taste. This is not true. Learn to use herbs and spices, but in moderation, so that you preserve the special quality and natural flavour of the food you are seasoning. In the interests of freshness, it is essential to replace your supply of ground spices at least every six months.

Although herbs and spices have been used in cooking and medicine for over 5000 years, there is still much to discover about their virtues. Many herbs and spices assist in the production of saliva and so contribute to an improved digestion. Recent studies have found that herbs belonging to the onion family such as garlic, onion, shallots and chives might help prevent certain cancers, while others such as coriander, fenugreek and onion are thought to be beneficial for those suffering from diabetes. Some, such as garlic, cloves, mustard and horseradish, have antiseptic properties and might slow down or stop the development of certain bacteria. Cloves, pepper, turmeric, ginger, nutmeg, sage and rosemary have antioxidant properties. Chillies vary in heat and intensity from the very mild to very hot, but need to be used in moderation as they can irritate the digestive system.

Many of the recipes in this book use herbs and spices, and you may enjoy keeping a few herbs in pots or in the garden to enhance your cooking. By getting to know the qualities of herbs and spices and using them for seasoning, you will learn to effectively cut down on the use of salt and oil in your cooking.

Notebooks

A notebook is a great learning aid and help to a cook. In her kitchen notebook, my wife, Angie, had jotted down recipes I cooked when we first met 20 years ago. If she hadn't done this, we would have forgotten some of our favourite dishes of the time. In my own notebook I have recorded some favourite recipes handed down by my mother and grandmother, as well as many dishes I have learnt in my travels and in my work as a chef. Most of them are now filed in a computer. In addition to actual recipes, I also record any special thoughts I may have, and ideas for different seasonings, cookery techniques, seasonal and special occasion menus and so on.

All this recorded knowledge may be of interest to relatives and friends. Many young men and women would value learning to cook from a more experienced cook, and I think our modern society could gain much from going back to the former tradition of passing on cooking knowledge from one generation to another. If the school curriculum taught young children the pleasures of developing their senses of smell, taste, touch and sight in relation to food, young people would be in a position to make better food choices, especially when also encouraged to contribute to family meals from an early age at home.

Shop for Fresh Food about Three Times a Week

The concept of one-stop shopping once a week has been promoted as highly convenient. I must admit I particularly dislike this idea for several reasons. First, shopping once a week forces you to plan what you are going to eat a long time in advance. Often it's far too much ahead. It is simply not exciting to know what you will eat in six days' time. By shopping once a week you are also forced to eat food that is not fresh for at least half of your meals. This is far from ideal. Sure, most of the grocery shopping can be done once weekly, but try to buy fresh food at least three times a week.

Following are some guidelines to remember. Eat fish, seafood and minced meat dishes or very thinly cut meats on the day you buy them. Meat cuts such as steak, chops and portioned chicken are best consumed within two days. Cook roasts within two to three days. The general rule is, the bigger the joint of meat, the longer it keeps. Buy vegetables and fruits three times a week – the fresher they are, the more nutritious they will be.

To my way of thinking, the freezing of fresh seafood and meats is necessary only when there is no alternative. Fresh is best.

Shopping lists

One of my favourite moments in the preparation of a meal is the time just before the cooking, when all the ingredients are assembled before me and I feel happy with them. On the other hand, everyone knows how frustrating it is to be ready to begin cooking and then realize that an important ingredient is missing.

A shopping list is of great help, and it is worthwhile including as much detail as you can to facilitate the shopping later. I prefer to write my list from my kitchen, where I can

Nuts and pulses are a
good source of protein

check what I need for the pantry, fridge and freezer. Even if you can't make up your mind on what you want to eat, it is still essential to check the pantry and fridge for basics such as oil, rice, spices and so on; then you can decide on your meal when at the market or shops. When I visit a market I have a good look first and sometimes sit down to finish my shopping list before actually buying anything.

At the top of the list I write a few important reminders like the fruits I need for the fruit bowl or the name of a particular dish. Then I make three or four columns with headings under groceries, fruit and vegetables, meat and fish and miscellaneous. Here is an example:

Breakfast food

Fruit for the fruit bowl

Sandwich fillings

Fish and green vegetables

Chicken and Vegetable Soup (for Saturday)

Pear and Prune Loaf (for Sunday)

Birthday cake for Michael

Groceries	Fruit & Veg	Meat & Fish	Misc
muesli	3 grapefruits	2 fish steaks	foil
skimmed milk	6 bananas	1.25 kg (2lb 12oz) chicken	baking paper
self-raising flour	1 lemon		
115 g (4 oz) ground	4 apples		**Baker**
almonds	2 pears		cake
cinnamon powder	4 oranges		bread
10 dried pear halves	1 mango		
10 dried apricots	450 g (1lb) broccoli		
20 dried prunes	900 g (2 lb) carrots (medium)		
4 dried apple rings	1 leek (medium)		
long-grain rice	1 bunch parsley		
cloves	1 bunch lemon thyme		
olive oil	1 head garlic		
6 eggs	green salad		
tuna in oil	1 avocado		
peanut butter	1 onion		
	2 tomatoes		

When cooking from a recipe such as the Pear and Prune Loaf that calls for 10 dried pear halves, 10 dried apricots and so on, you may have to buy more than you need, as dried fruits are often sold according to weight.

My list is just an example, and you'll enjoy making your list in your own style.

Visit a market for inspiration and knowledge

At the age of 16, I was lucky enough to be apprenticed to an extraordinary master chef, Albert Augereau, who took me several times a week to the Saumur market in the region of Anjou. He taught me the importance of smelling foods, touching them with respect and focusing on them to really see their beauty. Today I often take my cookery students to the market where they, too, can learn to recognize fresh produce, which is the backbone of a good dish. Just as visitors to an art gallery stand enthralled before a beautiful still-life painting, our senses are unconsciously stimulated in much the same way each time we visit a fresh food market. Just picture peaches, mangoes, cherries, strawberries, asparagus, bok choy and hundreds of other foods of all shapes, sizes, smells, textures and colours – they bombard our senses and interact with our brains.

When you visit a market you will be inspired to create meals from the available fresh, seasonal produce or dream of a new dish altogether. When I arrive at the market, I first stroll through the aisles, making a mental note of who has the best and most reasonably priced product. I don't hesitate to stop at a stall and closely inspect the ingredients before making up my mind.

Learn to recognize the best food suppliers

All food storekeepers, whether they be butchers, fishmongers, bakers or greengrocers, work very hard for many hours each week. The most dedicated greengrocers and fishmongers must be up in the early hours of the morning to get the best produce at the wholesale markets. They also have to establish and maintain a good network of contacts to ensure that they get a regular supply of first-rate produce. The best suppliers are busy, give good service and advice, and have a large turnover so the food is always fresh. There are, however, some busy stores with fast turnover and low prices which unfortunately sell food of an inferior quality, so you need to be vigilant.

To recognize quality and freshness requires practice. As an exercise, I suggest that you stop for a few minutes and have a good look at the display each time you pass a butcher, fishmonger or greengrocer. At the greengrocer's, look at the firmness and quality of the vegetables. Are the carrots unblemished? Is the cauliflower white? Are the greens limp? What herbs are on sale? Is the fruit carefully displayed? Look at the bananas. Are they a nice yellow colour, unblemished and just ripe? Or are they all green or over-ripe? Smell the fruits for sweetness and ripeness. Inspect the red fruits

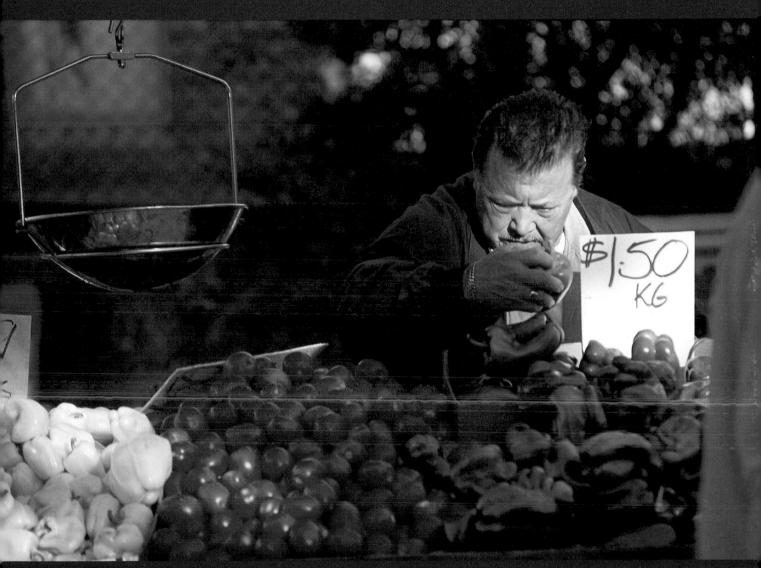

Visit a market for inspiration
and knowledge.

Try to eat fresh
fish several times
a week.

closely to see the quality. A good greengrocer always has several varieties of each vegetable, fruit or herb available.

At the fishmonger's see if there is a good selection of whole fish attractively displayed on ice, not piled on top of one another. Look at the texture of the fish. A fresh fish is firm and plump and has shiny skin with scales that hold together closely. It is a good sign if a shop sells delicate fish such as fresh sardines and red mullet, and seafood like fresh crabs, mussels and unopened oysters. A good fish shop offers both inexpensive family fish such as cod and plaice, as well as special-occasion fish such as salmon and Dover sole. Remember that the price of fish is usually not related to quality but rather to availability and demand. I have consistently found that markets are where you find the best fishmongers.

At the butcher's, see if the general display is neat and imaginative, and if the meat is well trimmed of fat and gristle. See if the steak, chops and meat fillets are cut neatly and evenly, and look for a bright meat colour in general.

Ask your butcher to show you how to trim the fat from meat.

Communicate with the people you buy from

Dedicated greengrocers, fishmongers and butchers have an extensive knowledge about what they sell and, more often than not, are happy to share what they know. When you realize that a shop has a high standard, let the staff know that you appreciate their work and compliment them on the quality of their produce. Every hard worker likes encouragement. Experienced storekeepers should be able to give you information on the provenance of the food, storage, cooking and serving tips to bring out the best in the produce.

Find out from the storekeepers about seasonal produce – there is a best time for everything. Not so long ago, one of my butcher friends told me that beef tends to be a little tougher in winter than at other times of the year. After 25 years of professional cooking, I still learn something every week from those I buy from, and I value their help so much.

In my experience, children also love visiting markets, so take them along if you can. If they help choose the produce and plan the dishes, chances are they will eat the food when it is cooked.

Markets exude such atmosphere – the interaction between people is inspirational, as are the discussions about food, and the lively exchange of recipes is invaluable. If you really have little chance of getting to a market, find out from friends who love cooking where they go for their produce.

Storing Food

Refrigerate perishable foods as soon as you arrive home. Store fish on the top shelf where it is coldest. Minced beef and other meats are stored in the meat tray, while vegetables go in the crisper at the bottom of the fridge (it is a pity that most crispers are so small). Do not leave vegetables wrapped in plastic. I keep bunches of fresh herbs, sprinkled with a few drops of water, loosely wrapped in freezer bags in the vegetable crisper. Make sure the refrigerator is kept clean and that unfresh foods are thrown out. If you are unsure about freshness, just smell the suspect item. The nose knows!

Store cooked food in the refrigerator as soon as it has cooled down, choosing a suitably sized container sealed with a well-fitting lid or covered with foil or plastic wrap. Avoid keeping cooked food for more than two days in the refrigerator. Freeze only fresh food or freshly cooked food (after it has cooled down) in airtight containers such as tubs or freezer bags, and use frozen food within a month or two of freezing. Store potatoes, onions, garlic and uncut pumpkin in a cool place away from the light. Store berries in the refrigerator, and keep less delicate fruits, such as apples, pears, bananas and oranges, in the fruit bowl.

The Pantry

It would be inappropriate to suggest that we should all keep the same foods in our pantry, for we are all so different. However, following is a list of convenient foods that are handy to have around, and which will help you whip up healthy meals in no time.

SPICES   Curry powder, pepper, cumin seeds, ground cumin, sweet paprika, chilli powder, coriander seeds, ground coriander, star anise, fennel seeds, cloves, saffron, cinnamon sticks, ground cinnamon, prepared mustard, vanilla essence, vanilla pods

OILS   Olive oil, groundnut oil, sesame oil and red-wine vinegar

PASTA, NOODLES, RICE   Make your own selection, including other cereals such as couscous and polenta

BREAKFAST CEREALS   Make your own selection, and try to limit the sugar-laden brands

PULSES AND BEANS   Lentils, cannellini beans, chickpeas (either dried or canned)

CANNED FOOD   Canned fish such as tuna and salmon, fruit, tomatoes

BOTTLED TOMATO SAUCE   This should be refrigerated after opening

CHINESE SAUCES   Low-salt soy sauce, oyster sauce, fish sauce, Chinese rice wine

NUTS AND SEEDS   Almonds, pinenuts, walnuts, and sesame seeds

The Refrigerator or Freezer

It is useful to always have on hand low-fat dairy products such as milk, yoghurt and cheese. I prefer using butter to margarine. Eggs, Italian-style tomato sauce, fruit juices and mineral water are important. Keep some bread, stocks and a few pre-cooked dishes for emergencies in the freezer.

1 Food mixer	7 Grater	14 Cast-iron grill	22 Conical strainer
2 Egg slide	8 Sharpening steel	15 Blender	23 Pepper grinder
3 Pasta lifter	9 Knives	16 Whisk	24 Scales
4 Skimmer	10 Oven rack	17 Serving spoon	25 Food processor
5 Flat oven tray	11 Roasting tray	18 Colander	26 Measuring jug
6 Multifunction saucepan: stockpot, steamer, pasta cooker	12 Wooden chopping board	19 Wooden tongs	27 Wooden spoon
	13 Pastry cutter and PVC pipe	20 Non-stick frying pan	28 Food mill (mouli)
		21 Casserole dish	29 Wok

Kitchen Equipment

The saying 'a craftsperson is only as good as his or her tools' is most applicable to cooking. Good cookware is of enormous benefit to any cook and helps save time, effort and, in the long run, money. My advice is to buy the best cookware you can afford; you won't regret investing in the things you need in the kitchen. If you cannot afford equipment that is used only occasionally, try borrowing it from family and friends.

The photograph on the opposite page shows a selection of recommended kitchen equipment. If you are just beginning to cook, don't feel you have to have everything. Start off with the basics: a few pans (large and small), a knife or two, a chopping board and a few small pieces of equipment, such as a strainer and wooden spoons.

Knives

Good knives are a cook's best friends. A good knife has balance between the blade and the handle, and a weight you are comfortable with. Ask for advice on how to store knives properly and how to take care of them. Chef's knives are usually the best to buy, and when you cook every day they are more than an indulgence. To do all kinds of small jobs, such as peeling and trimming fruits and vegetables, you will need a small paring knife with a blade of about 10 cm (4 in). A medium–sized knife with a wide blade about 20 cm (8 in) long is perfect for cutting vegetables and other foods. A boning knife has a thin but strong blade about 15 cm (6 in) long, and is useful for trimming fat from meat, portioning chicken and cutting fish into pieces. A serrated knife is useful for cutting bread and other slicing work. The good news is there will soon be good-quality knives on the market that require no sharpening. But in the meantime, to keep your knives sharp, you will need a sharpening steel.

Saucepans and frying pans

Buy the best saucepans you can afford and don't feel you need a complete set as there are sizes you may never use. Buy them individually and select pans with well-fitting lids. For low-fat cooking, non-stick cookware is highly recommended and the most useful pieces are a frying pan and a wide saucepan or casserole dish for casseroles and soups. A large stainless-steel steamer is terrific for cooking vegetables and can also be used to cook pasta, rice, soups and stocks.

Baking dishes, oven racks and grills

For roasting meat or baking, get a large, deep oven tray, preferably a heavy one so you can use it on top of the stove as well. An oven rack that fits into the roasting tray will allow the heat to circulate well around the food being roasted. A flat oven tray with a small edge is useful for baking fish fillets and vegetables. A cast-iron grill is perfect for grilling meat, fish and vegetables on top of the stove and can also be used in the oven.

Woks

What a fabulous cooking utensil the wok is! It can be used for stir-frying, boiling, steaming, casseroles, curries, soups and more. It is one of the best utensils to buy, and good value for money. Choose a thin but robust iron wok with a lid. The wok should come with a stir-fry spatula.

Food mixers, food processors and blenders, juicers, food mills and graters

An electric food mixer with a large metal bowl usually comes with three basic attachments: a balloon whisk, a beater and a dough hook. This piece of equipment makes bread, pizza dough, pastry, cakes and so on. Some food mixers offer other attachments such as a mincer, pasta maker or citrus juicer.

An electric food processor is another useful tool and offers several attachments for slicing and grating foods as well as one or more blades to mix, chop, blend or purée food.

An electric blender is ideal for blending soups into purées or just blending a liquid preparation. An electric juicer turns fruits and vegetables into superb drinks. A food mill (or vegetable mouli) is a hand-operated kitchen gadget for blending or puréeing food. It is good for soups and purées, and the best utensil for making mashed potato. A hand grater is essential for grating carrots, cabbage for coleslaw, and cheese; choose one that offers the most grating and slicing options.

Scales, measuring jugs and spoons

There are times when ingredients must be carefully weighed or measured and nothing is more precise than a set of electronic scales. In this book, a graduated jug with a capacity of at least 1 litre (2 pints) with graduations in millilitres (fl oz) is essential for liquids. For small quantities, the measures used in this book are standard:

> 1 tablespoon = 15 ml; 1 teaspoon = 5 ml

Other practical items include:

- A large colander for draining vegetables, fruits and pasta, and a fine strainer for straining sauces and sifting flour.

- Pastry cutters or PVC rings to help you shape food.

- Wooden spoons, fish slice, large spoons, skimmer, slotted spoon, ladle.

- A pastry brush to brush pans with a small amount of oil.

- A pepper grinder.

- A salad spinner to dry leafy greens.

- A bottle opener

Prepare mixed salads with a
variety of fresh seasonal greens.

COOKING & EATING FOR WELL-BEING

'Our food is our medicine', 'We are what we eat'. If we believe these two sayings, then the cook has a most important role to play in our well-being. In the role of the 'cook as doctor', a role that marries gastronomy with science, a good cook prepares delicious concoctions which 'service' all functions of the body. The medicine of a good cook gives more pleasure than that of the doctor, and acts as a preventer of disease and illness rather than as a cure.

To help us become thoughtful cooks, we need the aid of science. The Cancer Research Campaign and other health organizations have provided us with dietary guidelines with which we should all become familiar if we want to improve our cooking and eating for long-lasting health. Those dietary guidelines are spelt out here – this is not a fad diet, but a guide to encourage people to become better cooks and healthier and happier eaters.

Get into a Regular Eating Pattern

On several occasions in this book I talk about the benefits of learning from people who are older than us, who have a lifetime of experience behind them. From my grandmother, who lived until a hundred, and from my father, I learnt about the importance of eating proper, balanced meals at a regular time each day, meals that are modified according to my lifestyle.

Eating should be a pleasurable experience from the time you begin the meal until the end of the digestion of the food. Before a meal you should have an appetite, but if you have been starving for the past hour it either means that you did not eat enough nutritious food at the previous meal, or that you left too much of a break between meals. Try to get into an eating routine so that each meal keeps you satisfied until the next. If you must have a long break between meals, try to plan for a nourishing snack, such as a sandwich or fruit in between. Above all, avoid quick fixes like fatty foods or foods high in added sugar.

My grandmother often praised the habit of eating a light dinner in order to enjoy a good night's rest. Then, on waking, you are ready for a full breakfast that will take you to your next meal, and so on. The body does not appreciate too many snacks all the time; like us, the digestive system needs to rest. You will see that the body is like a clock and one of the bonuses of a regular eating routine is regular bowel movements.

Because eating is a moment of intimacy between us and our food, we should make time to eat and try not to eat on the run. Eating is a more pleasant experience physically and healthier for the digestive system if we are comfortably seated and not standing, walking or driving. I believe that noisy situations should be avoided. Where the noise levels are low, you can better appreciate the delicate and natural flavours of food. It has also been shown that people tend to choose foods that are saltier, sweeter and higher in fat in noisy environments. Think about that and test it out the next time you eat!

Take small mouthfuls and chew the food well to enhance digestion. Drink slowly. And whenever possible, share meals with those you love.

Listen to how your body feels after eating to get an indication of your digestion. Work out which foods, if any, cause problems, such as stomach burn, bad digestion, wind and so on. Establish the meals that make you feel good and those that make you feel uncomfortable. Avoid overloading the digestive system and learn to feel when you have had enough. Over a long period of time, finding out which foods suit you and which don't will keep you healthy.

Identify Bad Eating Habits and Slowly Change Them

I have an Italian friend who drizzles at least one tablespoon of olive oil over almost every dish he sits down to; every member of my family in France used to spoon at least three teaspoons of sugar into their morning cup of coffee; many people season their food with salt before they even taste it.

These three examples illustrate some common eating habits. Whether good or bad, such habits are inherited either from our cultural background, from the way our parents fed us, from peer pressure (children, adolescents, workplace), from those we currently live with or our lifestyle. To work out our eating habits, we first need to know about the recommended dietary guidelines and pay attention to the way we feel after eating and digesting. Following are some common inappropriate eating habits that need to be addressed:

- eating too few vegetables and insufficient fibre foods (bread, cereals)

- eating too much fatty food

- eating too much meat

- drinking too much coffee and sweet soft drinks

- drinking too much alcohol

- eating too many sweet foods

- eating too much salty food

You will have more success in changing inappropriate eating habits if you do it slowly. For example, if you usually put two teaspoons of sugar in your coffee, first cut it down to one-and-a-half teaspoons, then reduce it to one teaspoon, and so on. If you drink too much coffee, start by drinking a smaller cup, then alternate a cup of coffee with a glass of water or fresh fruit juice. Substitute rich snacks with fresh fruit, or drink freshly squeezed fruit or vegetable juice.

EAT A WIDE VARIETY OF FOOD

All health bodies, including the Cancer Research Campaign, diabetes organizations and government health departments agree that the most important guideline for a healthy diet is to eat a wide variety of foods. Those who love good food and those who cook could not hope for a better guideline, for it means that we can use all kinds of food in our cooking. Nothing is really considered 'bad'; everything is 'good' but always in moderation. The great advantage of eating a wide range of foods is that it supplies all the nutrients needed by the various parts of the body. All foods have a role to play.

Enjoy Plenty of Vegetables

I have noticed that most people enjoy vegetables more and more as they grow older. I personally love the textures, colours and flavours of vegetables, the way they are easy to chew and digest, and especially the way they make me feel at the end of a meal. They are simply good for us and have a positive effect on our health. In terms of volume, we need to eat vegetables in the greatest quantity. Vegetables are an excellent source of vitamins, minerals and dietary fibre. They help protect us against many cancers, especially those related to the digestive system, as well as many other diseases.

The challenge for our society is to ensure that young people enjoy and understand from a young age the value of vegetables. Take carrots, for example, one of the vegetables with the most goodness. They can be eaten raw, either whole as a snack, or grated in salads and sandwiches, or cut into small sticks and eaten with dips. Carrots can be sliced or diced for a soup or casserole. They can be stir-fried, steamed or puréed. Most children would enjoy carrots in at least one of these ways. Of course, parents ought not to force children to eat something they don't want, but try to understand that it may not be the actual vegetable but the way it is cooked – and the texture – that the children dislike.

Nutritional experts particularly recommend eating generous portions of yellow vegetables, such as carrots and pumpkin, green leafy vegetables, such as spinach and salad greens, and members of the cabbage family, such as cauliflower, bok choy, broccoli, brussels sprouts and Chinese broccoli. The fibre content of vegetables helps neutralize

There are many varieties
of Chinese vegetables
available these days, and
I think they are superb.

some cancer-causing substances, reduces the time the food stays in the intestine and helps reduce the absorption of fat by the body. (Excess fat is one of the factors that favours the development of some cancers and other diseases.)

In addition, the various vitamins and other chemicals present in vegetables play an important role in reducing the development of cancer. Some vegetables are known to counteract the toxic substances formed when meat and fish are burnt or overcooked.

Enjoy Several Serves of Cereals Daily

Cereals hold pride of place in all ancient societies, and the word 'cereal' itself takes its name from Ceres, the Roman goddess of agriculture. Cereals are a good source of complex carbohydrates, which provide long-lasting energy. Rice is the most popular cereal of all and remains an everyday food for over half the world's population. My Chinese friends claim to feel unwell if they don't eat rice for a few days, and some Italians are lost if deprived of their beloved pasta. Personally, I feel a bit unwell if I don't eat bread. Apart from rice, the other major cereals are wheat, oats, corn and barley. We should take every opportunity to consume some form of cereal daily. Having it for breakfast is an excellent way to start the day, and it is preferable that it does not contain extras like fats, sugar or chocolate. Enjoy mixed cereals with low-fat milk or soya milk. If a meal lacks cereal in the form of either pasta, couscous, or rice, substitute with a nourishing wholemeal or wholegrain bread.

Alternate Moderate Serves of Meat, Fish and Vegetarian Protein

Avoid consumption of large quantities of fatty red meat and try alternating with moderate servings of other lean meat, fish, dairy products, eggs, vegetarian protein and vegetables. Fatty diets are incompatible with good health. Most of us would benefit from eating fish two or three times a week, but avoid deep-fried fish and fish served with fatty or creamy sauces. Depending on your appetite, a moderate portion of fish is between 115–200 g (4–7 oz).

Trim away all visible fat from meat and remove the skin from chicken before cooking. According to the recently published COMA report on diet and cancer we should limit our daily intake of lean red meat to about 90 g (3¼ oz) per person.

Pulses such as dried beans, lentils and chickpeas are a superb source of low-fat protein and we would do well to eat them more often. It is best, however, to avoid eating a large quantity of pulses at one sitting as this may be hard on the digestion. A moderate serving of cooked pulses is between 85–115 g (3–4 oz). Pulses are best eaten with cereal foods, such as bread, pasta or rice as these foods complement one another.

It is good to eat nuts regularly but in very small quantities as they have a high fat content.

Eggs and dairy products are another source of protein that can be enjoyed in moderation as part of a varied diet.

Eat Several Serves of Fruit Daily

I was lucky growing up as a child in France: we had lots of fruit trees around our house so there was always fresh fruit all year round. We had pears, apples and various other fruits, and, being French, we often ate bread with fruit as a snack. Our modern society has unfortunately fallen into the habit of snacking on rich, processed foods that are high in sugar, fat and additives.

Fruit is a versatile food: it has wonderful flavour, great texture, needs no cooking and is so good for us. Always keep a well-stocked fruit bowl both at home and at work, and, most importantly, introduce your children to the pleasures of eating fruit with breakfast, lunch and dinner. Like vegetables, fruit is a great source of vitamins, fibre and other good things.

Consume Fatty Foods in Moderation

The average male's weight has increased by several kilos in the last decade. In fact, obesity is the most common nutritional disorder in the Western world.

Fat is the most energy-dense food, so if we consume more than we need, the extra energy will be stored as fat, resulting in weight gain. It is sometimes very difficult to know the fat content of some foods such as pastries, stir-fried dishes, deep-fried foods, cakes and chocolate bars. But we can learn to identify foods rich in fat by focusing on their taste and texture. If you feel you are consuming too much fat, try to cut down and ask for information about the food you eat at restaurants and take-aways.

Use a minimum of oil when cooking at home. Avoid deep-frying and use only a light coating of oil when pan-frying. Use a non-stick pan or wok when stir-frying: 1 tablespoon of oil is sufficient when stir-frying for two. All oils contain the same amount of calories. I use olive or groundnut oil, depending on what I am cooking, and butter for special occasions. Margarine is recommended as a substitute by the British Heart Foundation for those with a high cholesterol level. Basically, it is wise to consume butter, cream, cheese, other dairy products and margarine in moderation. Consider using low-fat dairy products and keep cream for special treats. Spread butter thinly on bread and try alternatives such as avocado, hummus, tahini and savoury nut spreads such as almond and hazelnut spread.

Salty and Spicy Foods

The family cook or cooks influences the way all members of the household eat. If we are regularly served salty food, we necessarily develop a taste for salt. In the long term excess salt can contribute to high blood pressure. Salt creates thirst and therefore discomfort, and excess salt only distracts the eater from the more subtle flavours of the food. Learn to cook using a minimum of salt and replace it with other seasonings such as herbs, spices and lemon juice. Avoid adding salt at the table before tasting the food, and read food labels carefully to ascertain salt content. Look out for hidden salt in cured and preserved foods.

Some sauces such as soy sauce, fish sauce and tomato sauce can be very salty, so take time to choose carefully when eating out. We are advised by the Cancer Research Campaign to consume smoked foods in moderation, as the smoking process creates substances which can be carcinogenic. Hot, spicy foods can increase the risk of problems in the digestive system when eaten in excess.

Moderate Sugar Consumption

The increasing prevalence of fast food – the gradual Americanization of the food we eat and drink – has had an impact on our overall sugar consumption. Refined sugar is a high source of calories and contains no nutrients other than carbohydrates. It is also a major cause of dental decay. Foods such as cakes, biscuits, desserts and chocolate bars contain a lot of sugar and fat. Go for fruits and low-fat savoury foods instead and limit these foods to occasional treats. Sugar in savoury foods also masks their natural flavours, so keep a check on its use.

Limit the consumption of sugar in coffee and tea. Choose cold drinks such as fresh fruit juices or water in preference to soft drinks with a high sugar content.

What to Drink and When

Water is the drink best suited to the human body, and an average person needs to consume 2.5 litres (4½ pints) of water a day. Ideally, half of that amount comes from the food we eat, especially in a balanced diet that includes plenty of plant food. The rest can come from plain, unflavoured water.

Fresh fruit juices are a good source of flavour, vitamins and water. When you are out shopping or working, try one of those juices available at some take-away outlets. Fresh fruit juice first thing in the morning is a particularly good way to start the day.

If your diet is not high in fat, plain milk is good in moderation. Otherwise, try skimmed milk or fat-reduced, protein-enriched milk. I tend to avoid milk when I have a cold as it seems to aggravate sinus congestion. Beware of flavoured milk drinks and milk shakes that have added sugar.

It seems that a new soft drink is created every month these days. However, these cordials, processed fruit drinks and cokes are high in sugar. They should be avoided, not only before meals because they cut the appetite for good food, but also in the evenings after dinner. I believe young children are better off without these drinks.

An intake of one or two standard alcoholic drinks per day such as two glasses of wine or beer is considered to be compatible with good health. If you are drinking alcohol, combine it with food to reduce the effects of alcohol on the body's metabolism. Avoid drinking on an empty stomach or between your last meal and bed time.

Excessive consumption of alcohol has been linked with many modern diseases, including cancer and liver disease. Alcohol is calorie-dense and contributes to diseases associated with obesity and malnutrition. If you know you drink too much alcohol, consider reducing your consumption slowly over time. Beer drinkers are encouraged to drink low-alcohol beer. If necessary, ask your doctor for help.

Coffee comes in different strengths and is a strong stimulant. It is best drunk in moderation. Refrain from drinking coffee on an empty stomach or in the evening after dinner. If you feel you are drinking too much coffee, alternate it with water, freshly squeezed juices or caffeine-free herbal teas. Like coffee, tea is a stimulant but not quite as strong. Drink tea in moderation and avoid it in the evening.

EAtING out & tAKe-AwAYs

Studies have shown that we are eating out more often and that our average weight is increasing. I believe that the two are related. Eating out in a restaurant or taking food away not only provides great pleasure for all, but also gives the cook a break and is a good source of inspiration – it is always nice to see how other cooks combine, season and present food.

All restaurants and take-aways try to please their customers in one way or another, in the hope of repeat custom. Unfortunately, restaurant and take-away food is almost always higher in fat, added sugar and salt than home-cooked food, and the choice of vegetables is too limited.

The restaurant industry needs to pay attention to this and, as consumers, we would benefit from making careful choices and demands when faced with a restaurant or take-away menu. While planning your meal, try to recall when you last ate and what you ate. If, for example, you are out for breakfast and your last meal was a rich dinner with wine, then avoid eating a rich breakfast and go for light, high-energy foods such as cereal, bread and fresh fruit.

When eating out, enquire about dishes that are low in fat – but beware, you may not always receive the truth. Ask about the size of the meal and what vegetables are served with it and in what quantity. Have a look around to see the size of the servings and read the menu carefully to find a dish that is delicious and nourishing. Learn to negotiate with the restaurant waiter or the person behind the counter at the take-away shop about adapting dishes to your needs. I often ask for less meat and more vegetables and for salad dressings to be served separately. It is all right to ask for smaller servings.

Watch for foods that have a high fat content such as: deep-fried foods of all kinds; dishes with a fair amount of cheese, including sauces; white sauces and butter and cream sauces; crumbed foods; chicken cooked with the skin on and meat that has not been trimmed of fat; some stir-fry dishes; processed meats such as salami; some dressings, including mayonnaise; food wrapped in pastry; pastries, biscuits and cakes; ice-cream and chocolate.

Watch the salt content as well: foods topped with lots of cheese; pickles, anchovies, cured foods; processed meats; dishes containing soy sauce, oyster sauce or fish sauce; food that is often automatically sprinkled with salt such as French fries and fried food.

Avoid eating several dishes containing meat protein in the same day. Choose dishes with plenty of vegetables and be very selective in the snacks you eat. When buying ready-made meals at the supermarket, read the ingredients carefully. Keep three-course meals for very special occasions.

You can be healthy and still eat a variety of foods. Take your time when you eat and learn to stop eating and drinking as soon as you feel you have had enough.

My 14 Tips for Cooking and Eating for Pleasure

1 Shop for fresh food at least three times a week and cook food at its freshest.

2 Develop a friendly relationship with fresh food people.

3 Stimulate your senses by looking at, touching, smelling and tasting new foods.

4 Take notes, write down recipes and share your cooking knowledge with those around you.

5 Eat a wide variety of foods and learn to cook new dishes regularly.

6 Enjoy plenty of vegetables, fruit and high-fibre foods like cereals.

7 Cook using a minimum of fat and consume fat and fatty foods in moderation.

8 Alternate meat, fish and vegetarian protein dishes.

9 Limit salty, smoked, sweet and hot spicy foods.

10 Drink alcohol, coffee and sweetened soft drinks in moderation.

11 Sit to eat and eat slowly.

12 Notice the content, taste, texture and effect of what you eat.

13 Watch your weight.

14 Learn to relax, exercise daily and enjoy life.

Soups are handy for the busy cook because they last for a few days and can be reheated as required. New cooks will be encouraged by the ease of preparing a simple soup. Plain single-vegetable soups such as carrot, pumpkin or broccoli, cooked with a little onion and water or stock, blended to a purée and seasoned with chopped parsley, chives or spices are really little trouble at all. A mixed vegetable soup where the vegetables are cut into small pieces and cooked together is also ideal if you want to use up the leftover bits and pieces in the fridge. Choose vegetables with contrasting flavours and texture, and either blend the cooked soup or leave it as it is. Adding potato, cooked beans, rice or small pasta transforms a soup into a light meal.

In this chapter you will find a few soup recipes containing meat or fish which can be served as a main meal. Whatever soup you make, serve it with good, fresh bread.

Asparagus Soup

Asparagus is a delicate vegetable,
so to retain all the flavour and goodness,
be careful not to overcook it.

SERVES 4

1 kg (about 2 lb) asparagus

1 teaspoon vegetable or
   groundnut oil

1/4 onion, finely chopped

1/4 teaspoon curry powder

1 small potato, very thinly sliced

1 litre (1 3/4 pints) water or chicken stock (p. 204)

salt and freshly ground black pepper

1 teaspoon butter (optional)

3 tablespoons chopped parsley

Peel the asparagus spears with a potato peeler if they are large, starting from just below the tip and descending to the base. Snap off the hard part at the base and discard. Wash the asparagus in cold water and cut into 2.5 cm (1 in) pieces.

Heat the oil in a saucepan and, on low heat, fry the onion for 2 minutes. Add the curry powder and stir well. Add the asparagus, potato and stock or water. Bring to the boil, season with a little salt and pepper, and cook for 10–15 minutes until the vegetables are just cooked.

Blend or purée the soup and pass through a fine strainer. Just before serving, stir in the butter and the chopped parsley.

Broccoli soup with a hint of curry

You can use all parts of the broccoli when making this soup. I enjoy this lovely vegetable soup with bread.

SERVES 4

2 teaspoons groundnut oil

1 small leek, finely sliced

1 teaspoon curry powder

1.25 litres (2 pints) chicken (p. 204) or vegetable
   stock (p. 203)

100 g (3 1/2 oz) pumpkin, peeled
   and cut into small pieces

1 kg (about 2 lb) broccoli, cut
   into small florets

salt and freshly ground black pepper

4 tablespoons chopped parsley

1 clove garlic, finely chopped (optional)

Heat the oil in a non-stick saucepan and stir-fry the leek and curry powder for about 3 minutes.

Add the stock and pumpkin and bring to a simmer. Add the broccoli, return to a simmer, and season with salt and pepper. Cook, uncovered, until the vegetables are soft.

Blend to a purée or pass through a food mill. Reheat the soup in a pan without boiling. Season with parsley and garlic before serving.

Pumpkin Soup with parsley & chives

You can make this soup with any type of pumpkin. Try substituting the cayenne pepper with spices like cumin or paprika – I think they are lovely variations.

SERVES 4

2 teaspoons olive oil

½ onion, peeled and chopped

1 kg (about 2 lb) pumpkin flesh, peeled and cut into small pieces

1 small potato, peeled and sliced

1.25 litres (2 pints) water *or* chicken stock (p. 204)

salt and freshly ground black pepper

2 tablespoons chopped parsley

a pinch of cayenne pepper

3 tablespoons finely snipped chives

Heat the oil in a saucepan and try the onion tor a few minutes. Add the pumpkin pieces, potato and chicken stock.

Bring to a simmer, season with salt and pepper and cook uncovered until the pumpkin is soft. This usually takes about 15 minutes.

Mash or blend the soup to a purée or pass it through a food mill. Reheat the soup in pan without boiling. Stir in the parsley and cayenne pepper and serve sprinkled with chives.

Leek & carrot soup

This lovely winter soup can be served as a light evening meal with bread if you've had a big lunch. You can make this soup using other vegetables such as broccoli or cauliflower.

SERVES 4–6

2 small leeks, white part only

2 teaspoons groundnut oil

2 medium carrots, finely sliced

1.5 litres (2¾ pints) water *or* chicken stock (p. 204)

salt and freshly ground black pepper

3 tablespoons chopped parsley

1 clove garlic, finely chopped

Cut the leeks in four lengthwise, leaving the root end intact to keep it in one piece while washing. Wash the leek thoroughly in lukewarm water to remove any grit. Slice finely.

Heat the oil in a large non-stick saucepan and on low heat gently fry the leeks for about 4 minutes, stirring constantly. Stir in the carrots, add the stock or water, and stir well. Season with salt and pepper.

Bring to the boil and cook for about 15 minutes. Blend or mash the soup to a purée or pass it through a food mill. Stir in the parsley and garlic just before serving.

Mixed vegetable soup

The liquid of this hearty soup makes a good vegetable stock. For a light dinner, sprinkle the soup with a little freshly grated parmesan and serve it with bread.

SERVES 4

1 tablespoon groundnut oil

1 leek, sliced

1 carrot, finely sliced

1 stick celery, finely sliced

½ small swede, finely sliced

¼ small cabbage, shredded

½ red or yellow pepper, diced

salt and freshly ground black pepper

1 clove garlic, finely chopped (optional)

3 tablespoons chopped parsley

Heat the oil in a non-stick saucepan and on low heat cook the leek, carrot and celery for 3 minutes. Add the swede, cabbage and pepper. Cover with cold water, season with a little salt and pepper and bring to a simmer. Cook for 20 minutes, uncovered.

Just before serving, stir in the garlic and parsley.

Lentil & Pumpkin Soup

This vegetarian soup is very satisfying when eaten with bread. If using dried lentils, soak them for 1 hour in cold water before cooking.

SERVES 4

2 teaspoons olive oil

½ onion, peeled and chopped

¼ teaspoon curry powder

4 baby carrots, peeled and finely sliced

1 litre (1¾ pints) water

100 g (3½ oz) pumpkin, peeled and diced

400 g (14 oz) can lentils, drained

salt and freshly ground black pepper

3 tablespoons chopped parsley

1 clove garlic, finely chopped

4 spring onions, finely sliced

Heat the oil in a large saucepan and on low heat stir in the onion, curry powder and carrots. Stir for about 2 minutes until the onions take on colour.

Add the water, pumpkin and drained lentils, bring to a simmer and cook until the vegetables are soft (about 15 minutes). Season with salt and pepper.

Blend half the soup to a purée. Return the purée to the pan and reheat without boiling. Stir in the parsley and garlic, and serve sprinkled with spring onions.

Minestrone

Most people love this classic Italian soup and, when eaten with bread, it is a satisfying meal on its own. Try to use fresh herbs for the best flavour. The soup will keep in the refrigerator for 3 to 4 days or for about a month in the freezer. When reheating the soup, bring it to a light boil for 2 to 3 minutes. If you are vegetarian, omit the bacon.

SERVES ABOUT 8

½ cup dried white beans, soaked overnight in plenty of cold water *or* a 400 g (14 oz) can cooked beans

3 tablespoons olive oil

1 onion, diced

3 cloves garlic, chopped

2 sticks celery, diced

1 carrot, diced

1 teaspoon finely chopped fresh rosemary

2 rashers lean bacon, trimmed and chopped

3 teaspoons tomato pureé

⅓ cabbage, washed and finely shredded

2 leeks, diced

3 courgettes, diced

1 tablespoon finely sliced basil

3 tablespoons chopped parsley

1 clove

salt and freshly ground black pepper

½ cup raw macaroni

Drain the soaked beans and place in a saucepan with about 2 litres (3½ pints) cold water (no salt). Bring to the boil and simmer until the beans are tender. This takes about 1 hour. Drain half the cooked beans and blend to a purée. Return the puréed beans to the pan with the whole beans. Alternatively, blend half of the canned beans and put aside.

While the beans are cooking, heat the oil in a large saucepan and gently fry the onion, garlic, celery, carrot, rosemary and bacon for about 10 minutes.

Dilute the tomato pureé with a little warm water and stir into the pan. Add the cabbage, leeks, courgettes, basil, parsley and clove, along with the whole and puréed cooked beans and their liquid. Add enough water to cover and season with a little salt and pepper. Bring to a simmer and allow to simmer for about 30 minutes.

Add the macaroni to the soup and cook for another 10 minutes. If you're not eating the soup immediately, allow it to cool completely before covering and storing in the refrigerator.

chef's note

Plan ahead when making this soup. The beans are best soaked overnight or for at least 12 hours. The preparation and cooking will take about 2 hours from start to finish.

chef's note

For the best results, use the freshest fish and prawns for this dish.

Fish & Prawn Soup with Fennel

This aromatic and flavoursome soup has superb texture and is a meal on its own.
Eat it with toasted bread brushed with a little olive oil and chopped garlic and, above all,
share it with good friends. Ask your fishmonger to clean and prepare the fish for you.
Preparation time is 1½ hours but I promise you the effort is worth it!

SERVES 4–6

12 fresh prawns in their shells

1 medium fennel globe

3 tablespoons olive oil

1½ litres (2¾ pints) cold water

½ medium onion, diced

10 cumin seeds

10 fennel seeds

½ small hot chilli

4 tomatoes, seeded and diced

1½ kg (3 lb) firm fish, such as monkfish, turbot or John Dory, cut into 4 cm (1½ in) thick steaks

salt and freshly ground black pepper

a pinch of saffron

2 small potatoes per person, peeled and boiled

1 clove garlic, chopped

Shell and devein the prawns, reserving the shells. Refrigerate the prawns while preparing the rest of the ingredients.

Trim off the feathery tops of the fennel, keeping only the globe. Cut the globe into 12 wedges.

Heat 1 tablespoon of the olive oil in a pan and stir-fry the prawn shells for 5 minutes until they change colour. Add the water to the pan and bring to the boil. Simmer for 20 minutes, then strain this stock into a bowl. Discard the shells.

Heat the remaining oil in a large saucepan and, on medium heat, fry the onion, cumin seeds, fennel seeds and hot chilli for 1 minute. Place the fennel pieces and tomatoes over the mixture, then place the fish pieces neatly on top of the tomato cubes. Pour over the prawn stock and, if necessary, add a little water so that all the ingredients are covered completely. Season with a little salt, pepper and saffron. Bring to the boil.

After 10 minutes, remove the fish from the liquid and add the prawns, potatoes and garlic to the pan. Keep on a low heat for 2 minutes (do not boil).

If you like, remove the bones from the fish. Place the fish and prawns on a serving dish and place the liquid with potato and vegetables into a soup tureen for everyone to help themselves.

Scallop & carrot soup

This is one of the very first recipes I concocted in the late seventies and I still love its simplicity and freshness. Insist on fresh scallops.

SERVES 6

1 teaspoon vegetable oil or butter

1 large shallot *or* ½ small white onion, peeled and finely chopped

3 medium carrots, peeled and grated

125 ml (4 fl oz) dry white wine (optional)

500 ml (18 fl oz) fish stock (p. 206) *or* water

salt and freshly ground black pepper

a small pinch of cayenne pepper (optional)

600 g (1¼ lb) fresh scallops

3 tablespoons chopped parsley

a few sprigs of chervil (optional)

In a large non-stick saucepan heat the oil and on low heat fry the shallots for 2 minutes without browning. Add the grated carrot and cook, stirring, for a further 3 minutes.

Add the wine and bring to the boil. Add the fish stock or water, and simmer for 5 minutes. Season with a little salt, pepper and cayenne.

Trim the scallops of rubbery bits and dark spots. Wash them briefly in water and drain immediately. Add to the carrots and return to a simmer.

Switch off the heat and leave to stand for 2 minutes. Serve sprinkled with parsley and chervil.

Crab soup with leeks & corn

This soup makes a delicious light meal when teamed with good, fresh bread. Save time by using canned crab meat and canned corn.

SERVES 6

2 medium to large leeks, white part only

150 g (5½ oz) crab meat, fresh or canned

1 teaspoon vegetable oil

1½ litres (6 cups) water

1 medium potato, peeled and diced

salt and freshly ground black pepper

400 g (14 oz) can sweetcorn, drained

1 egg, lightly beaten

2 pinches of cayenne pepper

3 spring onions, finely sliced

Cut the leeks into four lengthwise, leaving the root end intact to keep it in one piece while washing. Wash thoroughly in lukewarm water to remove any grit. Slice the leeks finely.

Remove shell or cartilage from the crab meat.

Heat the oil in a large saucepan on low heat. Add the leeks and stir-fry for about 5 minutes. Add the water and potato. Season to taste. Boil for about 15 minutes.

Purée the leek and potato preparation with half of the sweetcorn. Return to the pan with the crab meat and remaining sweetcorn, and reheat. Stir in the egg, season with a little cayenne pepper and serve sprinkled with spring onions.

Chicken & Vegetable Soup

This old European favourite can be made using a whole chicken or with your choice of chicken pieces on the bone. The broth serves as a soup either with the chicken and vegetables or just with the vegetables. Or you can cook some thin pasta in the broth and follow that with a main course of chicken and vegetables. The broth is also useful as a chicken stock.

SERVES 4–6

1.2 kg (2 lb 7 oz) chicken

3 carrots, quartered

1 leek, cut into sixths

2 sticks tender celery, cut into sixths

3–4 sprigs parsley

1 small onion, pierced with a clove

sea salt and freshly ground black pepper

3 tablespoons chopped parsley

1 clove garlic, chopped

Remove as much skin from the chicken as possible and cut off all visible fat (check the insides of the chicken too). Place the chicken in a large saucepan with the carrots, leek and celery. Add the parsley and onion pierced with the clove. Add enough cold water to cover all the ingredients, and season with sea salt and pepper. Bring to the boil.

Lower to a light boil. Skim off any scum that rises to the surface. After 45 minutes, remove the chicken from the liquid and cut into smallish pieces. Place the chicken in deep plates or bowls and sprinkle with chopped parsley and garlic. Discard the onion and parsley sprigs from the soup, and ladle the broth and vegetables over the meat. Serve with crusty bread.

SALADS

Salads are easy to make as most require little cooking. The secret of a good salad lies in the contrasting texture of the ingredients and, of course, in the dressing. Ideally, it is best to use a minimum of dressing to reduce the fat content in salads. Exciting flavours and effects can be added to a dressing with herbs (dill, parsley, chives, basil, chervil), nuts (walnuts, almonds, cashews, macadamias), spices (chilli, cummin, curry powder) and chopped garlic, onion, shallots and spring onion. Leftover rice, pasta and potatoes are also nice touches.

For the dressing, use good quality oils with strong flavours, such as olive, walnut or hazelnut oil, and for acidity use a good red-wine vinegar or fresh lemon juice. Make sure that the salad ingredients are well dried before tossing the salad with the dressing, and dress the salad just before you are ready to eat. When buying bottled dressings, read the list of ingredients on the label carefully. Have fun making your own concoctions, and enjoy good bread with salads.

Asian-style dressing

Try this dressing with a green salad, with mixed vegetables and meat or with a fish salad.

TO DRESS A SALAD FOR 2

½ small clove garlic, finely chopped

a pinch of castor sugar

juice of ¼ lemon

½ teaspoon sesame oil

¼ teaspoon chilli paste (optional)

2 teaspoons low-salt soy sauce

2 teaspoons groundnut oil

freshly ground black pepper

Whisk all the ingredients together in a small bowl.

French Dressing

Herbs and spices can be added to this simple dressing. Try adding parsley, basil, cayenne pepper or curry powder.

TO DRESS A SALAD FOR 2

½ teaspoon Dijon mustard

1 teaspoon red-wine vinegar

salt and freshly ground black pepper

1 tablespoon groundnut *or* olive oil

In a bowl whisk the mustard with the vinegar. Season with a little salt and pepper, then whisk in the oil until well incorporated. If you are adding herbs or spices, do so just before serving.

MEDITERRANEAN DRESSING

The flavours of basil, olive oil and garlic are superb with bitter salad leaves such as curly endive and radicchio.

TO DRESS A SALAD FOR 2

½ clove garlic, finely chopped

juice of ½ lemon *or* 1 teaspoon
  red-wine vinegar

salt and freshly ground black pepper

1 tablespoon olive oil

4 basil leaves, finely sliced

In a bowl whisk the garlic with lemon juice and a little salt and pepper. Whisk in the olive oil and the basil.

Low-fat cream cheese & yoghurt Dressing

This dressing is a good substitute for cream or butter, and is great with baked potatoes or steamed vegetables. Look for smooth low-fat cream cheese with a fat content of less than 8 per cent. Manufacturers call it quark or fromage frais.

TO DRESS A SALAD FOR 2–3

2 tablespoons low-fat yoghurt

3 tablespoons low-fat fromage frais

1 tablespoon low-fat milk

freshly ground black pepper

2 pinches of cayenne pepper

juice of ½ lemon

1 tablespoon snipped chives *or* finely
  chopped parsley *or* basil

Whisk all the ingredients together until smooth. Refrigerate if you are not using it immediately.

Tahini Dressing

Tahini is a flavoursome paste made from sesame seeds. It is available in jars at most supermarkets and health-food stores.

TO DRESS A SALAD FOR 2

2 teaspoons tahini

1 tablespoon water

juice of 1/2 lemon

salt and freshly ground black pepper

1/2 small clove garlic, finely chopped

Mix the tahini with water and lemon juice. Just before serving, season with salt, pepper and chopped garlic. If you wish to make the dressing thinner, add a little extra water.

Green Salad with Walnut Dressing

The secret of a good green salad is to include different varieties of green leaves. I like to add a few nuts to give the salad a little crunch. The dressing should be flavoursome. You can, of course, add other ingredients such as tomato or avocado.

SERVES 2

2 handfuls of mixed green leaves of your choice

1/2 clove garlic, finely chopped (optional)

juice of 1/2 lemon or 1 teaspoon red-wine vinegar

a small pinch of curry powder

salt and freshly ground black pepper

1 tablespoon olive oil

1 tablespoon walnuts, finely chopped

1 tablespoon finely snipped chives (optional)

Gently wash the salad leaves in a large amount of cold water. Drain and dry well using a salad spinner.

In a salad bowl, thoroughly combine the garlic, lemon juice, curry powder, a little salt, pepper and oil. Add the walnuts and green leaves.

Just before serving, toss gently and sprinkle with chives.

Potato Salad

This salad is ideal for a barbecue.
I use a dill and yoghurt dressing here,
but you can use your favourite dressing.

SERVES 2

6 small potatoes

salt and freshly ground black pepper

1 teaspoon Dijon mustard

1/2 teaspoon red-wine vinegar

1/2 tablespoon natural yoghurt

1/2 teaspoon low-fat sour cream

1 tablespoon finely sliced dill

1 tablespoon chopped parsley

Place the washed potatoes in a small saucepan. Cover with cold water and season with a little salt. Bring to the boil and cook for about 15 minutes or until tender. Leave under cold running water until the potatoes have cooled. When almost cold, peel the potatoes and dice or cut into slices.

In a salad bowl, combine the mustard, vinegar, yoghurt and sour cream. Season with salt and pepper and mix in the dill and parsley. Toss in the potatoes and serve.

Coleslaw with a Yoghurt Dressing

Using yoghurt instead of mayonnaise
makes this coleslaw a very healthy preparation.
This dish is excellent for barbecues.

SERVES 4

2 pinches of curry powder

juice of 1 lemon

4 tablespoons natural yoghurt

freshly ground black pepper

1/2 small white onion, finely chopped

1 tablespoon sultanas

1 tablespoon chopped cashew nuts

1/4 fresh, green cabbage, finely
   shredded or grated

1 medium carrot, peeled and grated

2 spring onions, finely sliced

To make the dressing, mix the curry powder, lemon juice, yoghurt, black pepper, white onion, sultanas and cashew nuts in a salad bowl.

Toss in the cabbage and carrot, sprinkle with the sliced spring onions and serve.

Bean & Artichoke Salad with sun-dried tomato dressing

This popular salad is ideal for a barbecue.

SERVES 4

300 g (11 oz) young green beans

4 basil leaves, finely sliced

2 sun-dried tomatoes, finely sliced

juice of ½ lemon

1 tablespoon olive oil

1 clove garlic, finely chopped

freshly ground black pepper

8 canned or bottled artichoke hearts, drained

2 tomatoes, quartered

Bring a large saucepan of salted cold water to the boil. Drop in the beans and cook until they are tender. Drain and dip the beans in icy-cold water to stop the cooking process. Drain again.

Place the basil and sun-dried tomatoes in a salad bowl. Stir in the lemon juice, olive oil, garlic and pepper. Add the artichoke hearts, beans and tomatoes to the bowl. Toss gently to distribute the flavours, and serve.

Sprouts & Mangetout Salad

Toss this salad in an Asian-style dressing. I like to use mung sprouts, but use the variety you prefer.

SERVES 2

100 g (3½ oz) bean sprouts

150 g (5 oz) mangetout, topped and tailed

juice of ½ lemon

¼ teaspoon sesame oil

1 teaspoon groundnut oil

2 teaspoons low-salt soy sauce

½ clove garlic, finely chopped

¼ red chilli, finely sliced (optional)

freshly ground black pepper

1 tablespoon sesame seeds

1 tablespoon finely snipped chives or coriander

Wash the sprouts and discard any blemished ones.

Place the mangetout in a bowl and cover with boiling water. Drain after 2 minutes and refresh in cold water. Drain again.

In a small bowl mix the lemon juice with the sesame oil, groundnut oil, soy sauce, garlic, chilli and pepper. Season the sprouts with half of this dressing and the mangetout with the remaining dressing.

Place the drained mangetout in the centre of a plate. Place the sprouts around the mangetout, sprinkle with sesame seeds and chives or coriander, and serve.

Beetroot & Bean Salad with parsley dressing

Use your favourite beans (borlotti, cannellini) for this salad. It is full of flavour and interesting textures. This dish is also ideal for vegetarians.

SERVES 3–4

3 tablespoons low-fat natural yoghurt

2 teaspoons red-wine vinegar

3 tablespoons chopped parsley

freshly ground black pepper

400 g (14 oz) can beans

2 or 3 beetroots, cooked, peeled and diced

2 spring onions, finely sliced

To make the dressing, combine the yoghurt, vinegar and parsley in a bowl. Season generously with black pepper.

Drain the beans and rinse them briefly. Add the beans and beetroot to the dressing and mix well to incorporate. Sprinkle with spring onions before serving. If you are not serving immediately, refrigerate the salad and take out 10 minutes before serving.

Waldorf Salad

The traditional Waldorf salad contains mayonnaise and cream. My offering successfully replaces them with a yoghurt dressing. The result is a light and delicious salad.

SERVES 3–4

1 tablespoon sultanas

3 tablespoons natural yoghurt

2 sticks celery, preferably from the centre, sliced

2 apples, diced

55 g (2 oz) chopped walnuts

freshly ground black pepper

juice of ½ lemon

a few lettuce leaves

Mix the sultanas with the yoghurt in a bowl. Add the celery and apple and stir well. Add the walnuts, pepper and lemon juice and stir again.

Line a salad bowl with the washed and dried lettuce leaves. Spoon over the salad and serve.

chef's note

Every French
family would
have a version
of this popular
summer dish.

Salade Niçoise

This is my version of a famous salad that originated in
Nice. More than a salad, it is a light meal full of flavour
and texture.

SERVES 6

2 medium potatoes

2 eggs

200 g (7 oz) young French beans

2 teaspoons red-wine vinegar

1 teaspoon Dijon mustard (optional)

salt and freshly ground black pepper

3 tablespoons olive oil

6–12 lettuce leaves, from the heart

2 tomatoes, sliced or cut into sixths or
  about 18 cherry tomatoes, halved

3 canned or bottled artichoke hearts,
  quartered

1 small brown or red onion,
  peeled and thinly sliced

200 g (7 oz) can tuna in oil

24 black olives, pitted

6 anchovy fillets, cut in half lengthwise

Wash the potatoes and place in a saucepan. Cover
with cold water, add a little salt and bring to the boil.
Cook for about 25 minutes until the potatoes are soft.
Remove from the pan and allow to cool in cold water.
Peel and slice.

Place the eggs in a saucepan, cover with cold water
and bring to the boil. Cover the pan, switch off the
heat and leave the eggs for 14 minutes. Remove the
eggs from the pan and place in a bowl of cold water
to cool. Peel and slice.

Top and tail the beans and add to a medium
saucepan of boiling water. Cook for 4–8 minutes until
the beans are tender. Drain and place in a bowl of icy
water to cool. Drain again.

Thoroughly combine the vinegar, mustard and a little
salt and pepper. Mix in the olive oil.

Line a salad bowl with the washed lettuce leaves. Add
the tomatoes, artichokes, onions, potatoes and beans.
Pour over the dressing and top with the eggs, tuna,
olives and anchovies.

Alternatively serve the salad in individual plates as
shown in the photograph opposite.

Tunisian Tuna & Egg Salad ·

This refreshing salad was inspired by a trip to Tunisia a couple of years ago.
The dish can be a light meal eaten with bread or an entrée for a warm-weather lunch.
For this recipe I use a North African chilli paste called harissa, available from gourmet
delis and some supermarkets. Use an Asian-style chilli paste if you can't find it.

SERVES 6–8

2 teaspoons red-wine vinegar
  or juice of 1 lemon

3 tablespoons olive oil

3 mint leaves, finely sliced

½ teaspoon harissa *or* Asian-style
  chilli paste (optional)

1 red or green pepper, seeded
  and diced

½ small globe fennel *or*
  ½ cucumber, diced

½ brown *or* red onion, diced

3 tomatoes, diced

salt and freshly ground black pepper

200 g (7 oz) can tuna in oil

2 hard-boiled eggs, sliced

1 tablespoon small capers

a few black olives

To make the dressing, combine the vinegar, olive oil, mint and harissa in a large bowl.

Toss the pepper, fennel, onion and tomato with the dressing and season to taste with salt and pepper.

Spoon the salad onto plates or a serving dish. Top with the flaked tuna, egg, capers and olives, and serve.

thai-style cabbage & bean sprout salad

It's worth learning to make this salad for the dressing alone.
You may wish to serve a grilled fish with it.

SERVES ABOUT 4

¼ Chinese cabbage, finely shredded

a handful of bean sprouts

10 cm (4 in) lemongrass stalk,
  white part only, finely chopped

juice of 2 limes *or* 1 lemon

1 tablespoon fish sauce

1 red chilli, seeded and finely sliced

1 clove garlic, chopped

1 teaspoon peanut oil

3 tablespoons coriander leaves

Bring a large saucepan of water to the boil. Cook the cabbage for 2 minutes in boiling water then drain. Refresh in cold water for a few minutes and drain again.

Wash and remove any damaged bean sprouts.

In a large bowl combine the lemongrass, lime or lemon juice, fish sauce, chilli, garlic and oil. Toss the drained cabbage and bean sprouts in the dressing and sprinkle with coriander leaves.

LIGHT M

snacks

eALS &

Whether having a snack at home or outside, the best
choice is one that will complement the other meals of the
day. Choose snacks that are high in long-lasting energy but
low in fat and sugar. The favourite snack of the Chinese is
a bowl of rice or noodles with a few vegetables or meat
or some broth, while Europeans tend to go for something
savoury on bread. Chocolate bars and fried foods are not
ideal snacks and parents need to influence their children
into making good food choices from a young age.
Excellent savoury snacks include salad sandwiches, soups,
low-fat dairy products, low-fat noodle, pasta and rice
dishes and low-fat, low-sugar breakfast cereals. If you
need something sweet, have a freshly squeezed fruit juice,
some fresh fruit or a slice of cake that has a low-fat, low-
sugar content.

Avocado & salad on Rye

A little avocado in a sandwich gives richness and smoothness and replaces butter or margarine in a satisfying way.

SERVES 1

2 large slices rye bread

¼ avocado

½ medium carrot, grated

½ tomato, sliced

a little alfalfa *or* shredded lettuce

salt and freshly ground black
   pepper (optional)

Place the bread on a chopping board and spread with avocado.

Top one slice with carrot, tomato and alfalfa. Season with salt and pepper, close the sandwich and cut in half.

Curried egg sandwich

This sandwich makes an ideal (and quick) lunch.

SERVES 1

1 egg

1 teaspoon olive oil or butter

a pinch of curry powder, or to taste

salt and freshly ground black pepper

2 slices wholemeal, wholegrain or rye bread

3 thin slices tomato

4 tablespoons finely shredded lettuce

Place the egg in a small saucepan. Cover with cold water and bring to the boil. Cover the pan, turn off the heat and leave for 14 minutes.

Remove the egg from the water. Shell and cool a little, if necessary. Mash the egg on a plate using a fork, then incorporate the oil or butter. Season to taste with the curry powder and a little salt and pepper.

Spread the egg on both slices of bread. Top one slice with the tomato and lettuce. Top with other slice of bread and cut the sandwich in half. *Bon appetit!*

chef's note

Wrap the sandwich in foil or plastic film if not eating within 15 minutes and refrigerate on a very hot day.

Tuna & salad sandwich

This sandwich is especially good on rye bread. Use your favourite canned tuna in olive oil.

SERVES 1

3 tablespoons canned tuna in oil, drained

4 tablespoons grated carrot

4 tablespoons shredded lettuce

freshly ground black pepper

2 slices rye bread

Break the tuna into small pieces and mix gently in a bowl with the carrot and lettuce. Season with a little pepper.

Spoon the tuna and salad onto one slice of bread. Top with the second slice, cut the sandwich in half and serve.

Beef burger & salad in a Roll

You can also use chicken for this dish. If you wish, season the meat with herbs and spices.

SERVES 1

a sprig of parsley, finely chopped

1 tablespoon cold water

125 g (¼ lb) lean ground beef

salt and freshly ground black pepper

a little oil

1 wholemeal roll

¼ avocado

3 tablespoons finely shredded lettuce

1 teaspoon mayonnaise (optional)

3 thin slices tomato

In a bowl and using your hands, thoroughly mix the parsley, water, mince and pepper. Form into a burger shape of about 2 cm (¾ in) thickness.

Brush a small non-stick frying pan with oil. Heat the pan and cook the burger on medium heat. Avoid pushing or moving the meat as it cooks. Cook for 3 to 5 minutes on each side, depending on how you like your meat, turning the burger halfway through. Season with a little salt if you wish.

Meanwhile, cut the roll in half and spread the avocado on each side. To the base of the roll add the shredded lettuce, then top with the burger, mayonnaise and tomato slices. Pop the top on the roll and serve.

Quick Pizza on Pitta

This popular snack is ready in 15 minutes. You can create your own toppings, using finely sliced vegetables of your choice. Use cheese moderately.

SERVES 1

1 small slice pitta bread

1 tablespoon grated low-fat cheese

1 small tomato, finely sliced

salt and freshly ground black pepper

2 mushrooms, finely sliced

1 teaspoon olive oil

Preheat the oven to 220°C/450°F/Gas Mark 7.

Place the pitta bread on an oven tray. Sprinkle a third of the cheese over and top with slices of tomato, overlapping slightly as you go. Season with a little salt and pepper and top with the mushrooms and the remaining cheese. Drizzle the olive oil over the top and bake in a preheated oven for about 10 minutes.

Nachos

Teenagers love nachos as a snack. The dish is often prepared using a Mexican-style tomato salsa available from supermarkets, but I have provided a simple recipe for a delicious salsa.

SERVES 2

¼ teaspoon chilli paste

¼ teaspoon ground cumin

1 teaspoon red-wine vinegar

1 teaspoon olive oil

1 large tomato, diced

350 ml (12 fl oz) Italian-style tomato sauce, bottled or home-made (p. 210)

2 spring onions, finely sliced (optional)

about 150 g (5 oz) plain corn chips

about 100 g (3½ oz) grated low-fat mozzarella

Preheat the oven to 180°C/350°F/Gas Mark 4.

To make the salsa, in a small bowl mix together the chilli paste, cumin, vinegar and olive oil. Add the diced tomato, tomato sauce and spring onions, and mix well.

Place the corn chips in a shallow ovenproof dish. Sprinkle with a third of the cheese. Top with the salsa and remaining cheese. Bake in the preheated oven for about 10 minutes or until the cheese has melted. Serve immediately.

Plain pizza dough

Making a pizza dough is like making bread dough. It is easier and
quicker when done in an electric mixer but try mixing it by hand once to develop
a 'feel' for the dough.

MAKES 2 LARGE PIZZA BASES OR 2 LARGE FOCACCIA

500 ml (18 fl oz) lukewarm water, made
with one third boiling water and two-thirds
cold water

2 teaspoons sugar

2 x 7 g sachets dry yeast

900 g (2 lb) unbleached, strong white
flour, sifted

1 teaspoon salt

3 tablespoons olive oil

Pour a quarter of the lukewarm water into a bowl and
add a pinch of sugar. Whisk in the yeast until dissolved.
Leave for about 5 minutes until the mixture starts to
bubble.

Sift the flour into a large mixing bowl. Add the salt and
remaining sugar, and make a well in the centre.

Add the remaining water and oil to the yeast mixture
and pour this into the well in the centre of the flour.
Incorporate the liquid into the flour either by hand or
with an electric mixer until it forms a thick sticky paste.
Mix well for about 2 minutes. Add a little extra flour if
the mixture is too runny, or a little water if it's too dry.
Cover the bowl with a clean tea towel and leave to rise
in a warm place for about 1 hour or until the dough has
doubled in bulk.

Flour the workbench and your hands and tip out the
dough onto the bench. Punch down. Divide the dough
into two or more pieces, depending on whether you are
making a small or large pizza. Shape the piece of
dough into a ball.

Rest the dough for about 10 minutes before rolling out
to make your pizza or focaccia.

Mushroom & olive Roll

This savoury roll is superb as a light meal served with a salad. The secret of the dish is to mix and roll the scone-like dough rapidly and to cook it without delay.

SERVES 6–8

1 teaspoon olive oil

400 g (14 oz) mushrooms of your choice, sliced

1 tablespoon tomato pureé

1 clove garlic, finely chopped

6 spring onions, finely diced

3 tablespoons finely chopped basil

55 g (2 oz) grated mozzarella

12 black olives, pitted and finely sliced

a pinch of salt

225 g (8 oz) self-raising flour

30 g (1 oz) butter

about 200 ml (7 fl oz) milk

1 egg, lightly beaten for glazing

Heat the oil in a large non-stick frying pan and cook the mushrooms until soft. Place the mushrooms in a bowl to cool. Mix the tomato paste, garlic, spring onions, basil, cheese and olives into the cooled mushrooms and season with salt.

Preheat the oven to 200°C/400°F/Gas Mark 6.

Sift the flour into a bowl and, using your fingertips, rub the butter and flour together until the mixture resembles fine breadcrumbs. Make a well in the centre and gradually stir in the milk to form a soft dough. You may need to add a little extra milk if the mixture is too dry or flour if it's too sticky.

Roll out the dough on a lightly floured surface to a 30 cm (12 in) square. Spread the mushroom preparation evenly over the dough and brush the edges with the beaten egg. Roll it up like a Swiss roll and glaze the top with the remaining egg.

Carefully transfer the roll to a greased baking tray and bake in the preheated oven for 30 minutes or until golden brown. Cut into slices and serve hot or cold.

Red Pepper & herb Bread

Serve this with antipasto at a barbecue or outdoor lunch.
It can also be baked as a focaccia or pizza base. You will need a greased bread tin.

MAKES 1 LOAF

1 tablespoon olive oil

½ red pepper, finely diced

1 tablespoon finely chopped fresh thyme

3 sun-dried tomatoes, finely sliced

12 Greek olives, pitted and finely sliced

1 teaspoon honey

4 tablespoons chopped parsley

450 ml (16 fl oz) lukewarm water, made with one-third boiling water and two-thirds cold water

2 x 7 g sachets dry yeast or 30 g (1 oz) fresh yeast

350 g (12 oz) unbleached plain white flour, sifted

115 g (4 oz) stoneground plain wholemeal flour

¼ teaspoon salt

Heat the oil in a non-stick saucepan and on low heat gently fry the pepper and thyme for about 4 minutes. Transfer to a plate and allow to cool. When cool, mix in the sun-dried tomatoes, olives, honey and parsley.

In a small bowl whisk half of the lukewarm water with the yeast until dissolved.

Place both flours in a large mixing bowl with the salt. Incorporate the yeast mixture and remaining water with the flour, using either one hand or an electric mixer. When the liquid and flour are combined, mix in the cooked vegetable and herb mixture. Cover the bowl with a clean tea-towel and leave in a warm place to rise for about 40 minutes.

Flour the work surface and your hands and tip out the dough. Knead with both hands for about 2 minutes. You will feel the dough becoming firmer and more elastic. Form the dough into a sausage shape to fit your greased tin, and place into the tin with the seam underneath. Leave to rise until the dough almost reaches the rim. This takes about 20 minutes.

Preheat the oven to 220°C/450°F/Gas Mark 7.

Bake the dough in preheated oven for about 35–40 minutes. Tip out onto a cake rack and check that the bread is cooked by tapping the bottom of the loaf. It should sound hollow. If necessary, return the loaf to the oven to cook a little more. Allow to cool before storing. The loaf keeps well for 2–3 days.

Mushroom medley on red pepper toast

Several types of cultivated exotic mushrooms like shiitake, chestnut and oyster are now available almost all year round. This dish is particularly lovely if you have access to wild mushrooms in autumn.

SERVES 6

300 g (11 oz) mushrooms, mixed varieties of your choice

3 tablespoons olive oil

1 shallot, finely chopped

1 clove garlic, finely chopped

2 tablespoons chopped parsley

salt and freshly ground black pepper

6 large slices of red pepper and herb bread, toasted (p. 71)

Rinse the mushrooms briefly and slice.

Heat the oil in a non-stick frying pan and sauté the mushrooms and shallots until the mushrooms are cooked. Stir in the garlic and parsley and season with salt and pepper.

Serve on slices of hot toast.

Focaccia with olives & thyme

Focaccia is a flat Italian bread usually seasoned with herbs, spices and vegetables. Serve this as an antipasto or a light lunch. You need a greased oven tray (or two) to hold the focaccia.

MAKES 2 LARGE FOCACCIA (8–12 SLICES)

1 quantity of plain pizza dough (p. 69)

3 tablespoons olive oil

freshly ground black pepper

1 tablespoon chopped fresh lemon thyme

2 cloves garlic, finely chopped

about 16 Greek olives, pitted and halved lengthwise

100 g (3½ oz) low-fat mozzarella, grated

Preheat the oven to 240°C/475°F/Gas Mark 9.

Divide the pizza dough in half and press or roll out the two pieces of dough to a circle or oval of about 2 cm (¾ in) thickness.

In a small bowl, mix together the olive oil, pepper, thyme and garlic. Brush this mixture over the dough and press in the olive halves. Sprinkle with the cheese and bake in a preheated oven for about 10 minutes or until cooked. The base must be browned.

chef's note

Excellent focaccia toppings include sun-dried tomatoes, anchovies, onion rings and various cheeses. Avoid too many salty seasonings.

Baked eggs & tomato

This dish is good with a mixed vegetable salad. You will need 2 individual porcelain or pottery soufflé moulds. If you wish, replace the tomato with ratatouille (p. 119), the popular vegetable dish from the south of France.

SERVES 1

a little olive oil to grease the soufflé moulds

4 slices tomato, about 1 cm (⅓ in) thick or 4 tablespoons Italian-style tomato sauce, bottled or home-made (p. 210)

about 3 basil leaves or parsley or tarragon, fincly chopped

2 medium eggs

salt and freshly ground black pepper

Grease the soufflé moulds with olive oil.

Place 2 cm (¾ in) of hot water in an oven dish. Preheat the oven to 180°C/350°F/Gas Mark 9.

Place one tomato slice or 1 tablespoon Italian tomato sauce in each soufflé mould and sprinkle with the basil. Break an egg over the top and season with a little salt and pepper. Top with the remaining tomato slices or sauce, and season with more pepper.

Stand the moulds in the hot water and bake in the oven for about 5 minutes, or a little longer if you like the yolk more cooked.

Omelette with mushrooms & Herbs

This dish can be adapted to suit your taste and what you have in the refrigerator. Use a non-stick frying pan.

SERVES 1

2 eggs

1 teaspoon vegetable oil

1 teaspoon butter or olive oil

115 g (4 oz) sliced mushrooms

about 50 g (almost 2 oz) bean sprouts (optional)

2 spring onions, sliced

2 teaspoons sliced coriander leaves

salt and freshly ground black pepper

Beat the eggs in a bowl.

Heat the oil and butter in a non-stick frying pan and fry the mushrooms for about 3 minutes. Add the bean sprouts and stir for 20 seconds before adding the beaten eggs, spring onions, coriander leaves and a little salt and pepper. Stir the egg gently in the pan to enable it to cook quickly. Serve hot when the eggs have set.

Fried eggs with ratatouille

This is the kind of light meal I enjoy with bread when I am cooking for one.
You only need a small frying pan to prepare this.

SERVES 1

1 teaspoon olive oil

a sprig of thyme, chopped

¼ onion, peeled and diced

¼ red pepper, diced

1 small courgette, diced

¼ small aubergine, diced

1 tomato, diced

salt and freshly ground black pepper

a pinch of cayenne pepper

1 or 2 eggs

Heat the olive oil in a small non-stick frying pan. Add thyme and onion to the pan and stir for 1 minute. Add the pepper, stir for a further minute then add the courgette, aubergine and tomato. Cook until the vegetables are soft. This takes about 5–10 minutes. Season with salt, pepper and cayenne.

Make a hollow in the centre of the vegetables. Break the egg into the centre, cover the pan and cook until the white of the egg has set. Season the egg yolk with black pepper and serve immediately.

Vegetable samosas

I use ready-made filo pastry to make these delicious vegetable parcels. To make neat samosas, it is preferable to use two layers of filo at a time. You can assemble the samosas ahead of time and cook them at the last minute. You will need 2 greased baking sheets.

MAKES ABOUT 15 SAMOSAS

1 tablespoon groundnut oil

¼ onion, chopped

1 clove garlic, chopped

1 teaspoon grated ginger

½ red pepper, finely diced

1 tomato, finely diced

½ teaspoon curry powder

½ teaspoon turmeric

¼ teaspoon chilli paste

½ teaspoon cumin

1 medium carrot, peeled and steamed or boiled until soft

1 medium yellow sweet potato, peeled and steamed or boiled until soft

115 g (4 oz) shelled peas, cooked

10 sheets filo pastry

Heat the oil in a medium saucepan and fry the onion, garlic and ginger until transparent.

Add the pepper and tomato and cook on low heat for about 5 minutes, stirring from time to time. Add the curry powder, turmeric, chilli paste and cumin, and cook for an extra minute.

Dice the cooked carrot and sweet potato and mix with the pepper and tomato preparation. Leave the vegetables to cool.

Brush the two baking sheets with a little oil and preheat the oven to 200°C/400°F/Gas Mark 6.

Place two sheets of filo on top of each other with the narrow side towards you. Cut in three lengthwise. Place 1 tablespoon of the cold vegetables at the base of one of the long rectangles of double filo, about 2 cm (¾ in) inside the edge. Now fold the bottom right-hand corner over to meet the left-hand side of the rectangle. This forms a small triangle at the base. Continue folding the triangle over upon itself, bottom corner towards opposite side, until you reach the top. Make the rest of the samosas in the same way.

Place the samosas on oiled baking sheet and brush the top of each with a little oil. Cook in a preheated oven for 15–20 minutes until golden.

Wholemeal Bread

We enjoy this quick-and-easy bread toasted for breakfast and in sandwiches.

MAKES 1 LOAF

350 g (12 oz) stoneground wholemeal flour

175 g (6 oz) unbleached white flour

55 g (2 oz) soya flour

3 tablespoons unprocessed bran

½ teaspoon salt

1 tablespoon molasses

1 tablespoon groundnut oil

500–600 ml (18–20 floz) warm water

30 g (about 1 oz) fresh yeast

Place the three types of flour, bran and salt in a large bowl with the molasses and oil.

Add half of the warm water to a second bowl. Crumble the yeast into the water and whisk until dissolved. Add the remaining water to the yeast mixture.

If you are using a food mixer, attach the dough hook, and mix the flour and the liquid little by little until the dough forms a ball and comes away from the side of the bowl. If you are mixing by hand, work the yeasty liquid into the ingredients in the large bowl, gradually incorporating the remaining water until the dough comes away from the side of the bowl. This takes about 1 minute. Cover with a tea-towel and leave to rise for about 30–45 minutes.

Flour your hands and the work surface to prevent the dough from sticking and remove from the bowl. Knead hard with both hands for about 2 minutes.

Form the dough into a sausage shape to fit your greased tin and place in the tin with the seam underneath. Leave to rise until the dough comes to just above the rim of the tin. This takes about 20 minutes.

Preheat the oven to 220°C/450°F/Gas Mark7.

Bake the bread in a preheated oven for about 35–40 minutes. When cooked, the sides of the bread are a golden brown colour and the bottom of the loaf should make a hollow sound when tapped. If necessary, return it to the oven. Tip the bread onto a cake rack to cool. The loaf keeps for 2–3 days.

chef's note

To make the bread lighter, I have used a ratio of one-third plain white flour to two-thirds wholemeal flour, but these proportions may be altered to suit your own taste.

Smoked salmon & Avocado parcels.

These parcels make a lovely special occasion entrée or light main course.
You can use a small porcelain cup measuring about 6 cm (2½ in) in diameter
to help you form the parcel.

MAKES 8 PARCELS

1 ripe tomato, diced

1 avocado, diced

1 small shallot *or* ¼ onion, chopped

juice of 1 lemon

1 tablespoon finely chopped dill

salt and freshly ground black pepper

a pinch of cayenne pepper

8 large slices of smoked salmon
   or 16 smaller ones

1 tablespoon olive oil

200 g (7 oz) leafy greens

about 25 cherry tomatoes

sprigs of dill and wedges of lemon

In a medium bowl gently combine the tomato, avocado, shallots, half the lemon juice, dill, salt, pepper and cayenne pepper.

Line the inside of a small cup with a 20 cm (8 in) square piece of plastic film. Line the plastic with one large slice or two smaller slices of smoked salmon. Place half a tablespoon of the avocado preparation into the centre of the salmon and carefully fold the plastic around the salmon to form a tight parcel. Set aside and make the other parcels in the same way. Carefully peel off the plastic from the salmon. Refrigerate until required.

To make the dressing, combine the remaining lemon juice, olive oil and a little black pepper.

Place the leafy greens onto a large platter or divide into individual serving plates. Pour over the dressing. Place the salmon parcels onto the bed of greens, and garnish with the cherry tomatoes and dill. Squeeze over some lemon juice, and serve with any remaining avocado and tomato.

Fresh fruit & vegetable juice

Fruit and vegetable juices have become more popular in the past 20 years, and for good reason. Fresh juice makes an excellent drink and nourishing snack. The juice you make yourself is also much nicer than the store-bought variety, and it's so easy if you own an electric juicer.

I believe that to derive the most pleasure we should sip rather than gulp down juices. Avoid sweetening fresh fruit juice; if you must, add one teaspoon of honey for this purpose. To prepare fruit for juicing, wash the fruit well and remove any pips or stone. Peel citrus fruits and remove all the pith. It is a good idea to sprinkle a little lemon juice over delicate cut fruits such as pears and nectarines to prevent them from turning brown.

Apple & carrot juice

Apples and carrots are both full of vitamins and goodness. By juicing them you will get the most out of their nutritional value since the vitamins are more readily absorbed into the system.

SERVES 1

1 large carrot

1 large Granny Smith or other apple of your choice

Wash the carrot and cut into small pieces to fit your juicer. Wash, quarter and core the apple. Cut into pieces.

Feed the carrot and apple pieces through the juicer and serve immediately.

Pear, Apple & Ginger Juice

This is a refreshing, spicy fruit juice, but avoid using too much ginger.

SERVES 1

1 ripe pear such as Williams

1 apple such as Granny Smith

1/4 lemon

1/2 cm (3/10 in) slice of ginger

Wash, quarter and core the pear and apple. Cut into pieces to fit your juicer.

Peel the lemon and ginger.

Feed the pear, apple, lemon and ginger into a juicer and drink the juice immediately.

Melon Juice

This is a very refreshing drink, especially on
a hot day. If you're unable to get all three types
of melon, just replace with one of the others.

SERVES 1

100 g (3½ oz) watermelon flesh

100 g (3½ oz) canteloupe melon flesh

100 g (3½ oz) honeydew melon flesh

Cut or scoop out the melon flesh. Discard the pips
and cut the flesh into pieces to fit your juicer. Feed
through the juicer. Add a few ice-cubes to the
juice, if you wish, and drink immediately.

Tomato, celery & carrot Juice

Make this delicious juice using
a ripe tomato and young carrots.

SERVES 1

1 tomato

2 baby carrots

1 tender stick celery

Wash the tomato, carrots and celery and cut into
small pieces. Feed through the juicer and drink
immediately.

vegeta

dishes

We have such a huge variety of plant foods such as vegetables, pulses, cereals, nuts, herbs and fruits, that with just a little knowledge it is possible to create many delicious vegetarian dishes. Studies have shown that there is a lower incidence of obesity, high blood pressure, heart disease and cancers among vegetarians.

For a vegetarian dish to be a complete meal it needs to provide a combination of two types of plant food protein. Cereal grains such as wheat, oats and rice, nuts and seeds provide one type of protein, while legumes such as dried beans, lentils and chickpeas provide the rest. A dish of baked beans on wholegrain toast is a good example of a combination of the two plant food proteins.

Eggs and dairy products are an excellent source of protein. Ultimately, a vegetarian diet must be varied to provide all the nutrients the body needs. Dietary experts tell us that it is beneficial for us all to alternate meat, fish and vegetarian protein in our diet.

Hummus

Hummus is a Middle-Eastern dip that is delicious served as an antipasto with raw vegetables or as a sauce for fish and grilled vegetables. It is quite readily available from gourmet food shops but it is as easy to make your own. You can use canned chickpeas or cook your own for this recipe. This dip keeps for 3 to 4 days, refrigerated.

SERVES 4–6

250 g (9 oz) cooked chickpeas

1 teaspoon ground cumin

2 pinches of salt

3 tablespoons tahini (sesame-seed paste)

juice of 1 lemon

4 tablespoons water

freshly ground black pepper

1 clove garlic, very finely chopped

Blend the chickpeas to a fine purée. Add the cumin, salt, tahini, lemon juice, water and a little pepper, then blend again. Refrigerate and, just before serving, add the chopped garlic.

Puréed beans with coriander

This delicious purée is a practical dish for vegetarians. Try it on toast or use it as a spread for pizza or vegetarian tartlets. It can also be served simply with steamed vegetables. For this recipe, I use canned beans. The purée keeps well for 3 to 4 days in the fridge.

SERVES 2–3

400 g (14 oz) can plain beans such as cannellini or borlotti

1 tablespoon olive oil

¼ teaspoon cumin

¼ teaspoon chilli paste

salt and freshly ground black pepper

about 10 coriander leaves, finely sliced

In a small saucepan reheat the beans in their liquid for a few minutes. Drain and discard the liquid.

Blend the drained, cooked beans to a purée with the olive oil, cumin and chilli paste. Season. Stir in the coriander and serve.

chef's note

Unlike other foods like pasta and rice, do not season dried beans at the beginning of the cooking as salt makes them tough.

Salad of lentils, cherry tomatoes & Apple

If you have time, soak the lentils for several hours before cooking them.

SERVES 4

175 g (6 oz) brown lentils

12 cumin seeds (optional)

a pinch of curry powder

salt and freshly ground black pepper

1 teaspoon red-wine vinegar

1 tablespoon olive oil

250 g (9 oz) cherry tomatoes, halved or left whole

1 Granny Smith apple, peeled and diced

½ small onion, chopped

3 tablespoons chopped parsley

Soak the lentils for at least 30 minutes then drain. Place the lentils in a saucepan with the cumin seeds. Cover with three times their volume of water and bring to the boil. Simmer for about 30 minutes or until tender. If necessary, add a little water during cooking, but allow the liquid to evaporate towards the end. There should be very little liquid remaining when the lentils are cooked. Allow to cool.

To make the dressing, in a small bowl, mix together the curry powder, salt and a little pepper with the vinegar. Slowly add the oil.

Place the cold lentils, cherry tomatoes and apple in a salad bowl and toss with the dressing, onion and parsley.

Home-made baked beans

I realize how much easier it is to open a can, but the beans you cook yourself are much more delicate and tasty. Choose the dried beans you like best and soak them overnight in a large quantity of cold water. When cooked, the beans keep well in the fridge for 3 to 4 days or in the freezer for 1 month.

SERVES 4

175 g (6 oz) dried beans such as cannellini, soaked
  overnight or for at least 12 hours

1 small onion, halved

2 cloves garlic, peeled and left whole

a few sprigs of parsley

½ bay leaf

a sprig of thyme

1 teaspoon tomato pureé

250 ml (8 fl oz) Italian-style tomato sauce, bottled or home-made (p. 210)

salt and freshly ground black pepper

Drain the soaked beans and place in a saucepan with the onion, garlic, herbs, tomato pureé and tomato sauce. Cover with water and bring to the boil.

Simmer until the beans are tender. Discard the onion, garlic and herbs and season with a little salt and pepper. Serve on your favourite toasted bread.

Vegetarian Risotto

I use a rich vegetable stock to cook this beautiful dish. If you wish, the parmesan can be replaced with 2 tablespoons of pumpkin purée or 1 tablespoon of crunchy peanut butter. Use a short, round-grain Italian rice such as Arborio for this dish.

SERVES 2

350 ml (12 fl oz) vegetable stock (p. 203)

100 g (3½ oz) mushrooms, finely sliced

1 tablespoon olive oil

½ onion, finely chopped

½ carrot, finely chopped

10 cm (4 in) stick celery, finely chopped

½ cup risotto rice

100 g (3½ oz) spinach leaves, washed

1 tablespoon freshly grated parmesan

salt and freshly ground black pepper

Bring the vegetable stock and mushrooms to the boil, then reduce the heat and keep it simmering while making the risotto. Strain off the mushrooms and set aside.

Heat the oil in a medium saucepan and gently fry the chopped vegetables for about 4 minutes until soft. Add the rice and mix well for about 1 minute. Add about half a cup of stock to the rice and, while stirring, bring to a simmer. When almost all the stock has been absorbed, add another quarter cup of stock and gently stir. Keep on adding the stock, a quarter cup at a time, until the rice is cooked, but still with a firm bite in the centre. You may either have a little stock leftover or you may run out of stock, in which case use some boiling water.

Two minutes before the rice is ready, add the mushrooms and spinach. While stirring, add the parmesan and season. Taste a few grains of rice to check if it is cooked. At this point, the preparation will be creamy but not runny. Cover the risotto with a lid and allow it to rest for about 3 minutes before serving. The entire cooking process should take about 18–20 minutes.

Noodle, vegetable & spiced dried beancurd soup

This soup is the kind of meal I really love and I sometimes prepare it when on my own. The spiced dried beancurd comes in vacuum-packed plastic packs, usually containing 4 to 6 squares of beancurd. Both the beancurd and egg noodles are readily available from the refrigerated section of Chinese grocery shops and supermarkets.

SERVES 2

2 teaspoons groundnut oil

2 squares spiced dried beancurd, cut into matchstick-size strips

2 large slices ginger

1 stick celery, cut into long, thin strips

1 medium carrot, cut into long, thin strips

100 g (3½ oz) shiitake mushrooms *or* other mushrooms of your choice

1 litre (1¾ pints) water *or* vegetable stock (p. 203)

2 branches Chinese broccoli, cut diagonally into 4 cm (1¾ in) pieces

200 g (7 oz) fine Chinese egg noodles

2 teaspoons soy sauce

½ small chilli, finely sliced (optional)

50 g (2 oz) bean sprouts, washed

2 spring onions, finely sliced

Heat a wok and add half the oil. When the oil is hot, add the dried beancurd and stir-fry for 30 seconds. Transfer to a plate.

Heat the remaining oil and add the ginger, celery, carrot and mushrooms and stir-fry for 30 seconds. Add the stock, bring to the boil and allow to simmer for 5 minutes. Add the Chinese broccoli and bring to the boil for 2 minutes.

In the meantime, place the egg noodles in a bowl and pour over boiling water from the kettle. Drain the noodles after 2 minutes and add to the soup. Add the soy sauce and chilli, and spoon over the spiced beancurd and bean sprouts. Sprinkle with the spring onions and serve.

Vegetarian Pizza

This pizza is made with a home-made pizza base. As an alternative to making your own, you can either buy some bread dough from a baker or buy a ready-made pizza base from a supermarket or gourmet food shop.

MAKES 2 LARGE PIZZAS OR 8 SMALL PIZZAS

2 courgettes, sliced lengthwise

1 small aubergine, cut into rounds

3 tablespoons olive oil

200 g (7 oz) mushrooms, sliced

100 g (3½ oz) baby spinach leaves, washed

1 quantity of plain pizza dough (p. 69)

2 cloves garlic, finely chopped

1 teaspoon finely chopped fresh thyme

freshly ground black pepper

a pinch of chilli pepper

150 ml (¼ pint) Italian-style tomato sauce, bottled or home-made (p. 210)

100 g (3½ oz) grated low-fat mozzarella

8–12 canned or bottled artichoke hearts, halved

8 Greek olives, pitted and halved

Brush the courgettes and aubergine with a little olive oil and cook on a hot grill or in a non-stick frying pan until soft. Transfer to a plate. Grill or pan-fry the mushrooms until soft. Transfer the mushrooms to a plate. Cook the spinach until soft.

Preheat the oven to 240°C/475°F/Gas Mark 9.

Cut the pizza dough according to the number of pizzas you are preparing. Form the dough into balls and roll out into round pizza bases of about 1 cm (⅓ in) thickness or less. The dough can be stretched by pulling it gently. Place the pizza bases on greased oven trays.

In a small bowl mix the remaining olive oil with the garlic and thyme. Season with a little pepper and a pinch of chilli pepper. Brush the dough with this seasoned oil and spread a little tomato sauce on top. Sprinkle some of the cheese over the top and add the cooked spinach, mushrooms, courgettes, aubergine and artichokes. Sprinkle with the remaining cheese and press in the olive halves.

Cook the pizzas in the preheated oven for about 15–20 minutes until the base is dry and lightly browned underneath.

Stir-fried spiced beancurd with young beans

You will find spiced beancurd in the refrigerated section at Asian foodstores. It usually comes in vacuum-packed sachets containing 4 or 6 squares of beancurd. Garlic chives are also readily available from Asian foodstores. The quantities of vegetables here can be easily varied according to your taste.

SERVES 2

2 teaspoons groundnut oil

250 g (9 oz) fresh young beans, topped, tailed and cut diagonally into 3 cm (1½ in) pieces

3 tablespoons water

2 squares spiced beancurd, cut into matchstick-size pieces

4 tablespoons garlic chives, cut into 3 cm (1½ in) pieces

⅓ of a small red hot chilli, finely sliced

½ teaspoon sugar

2 teaspoons light soy sauce

Heat a wok and add the oil. Add the beans and stir-fry for 10 seconds. Add the water, cover with a lid and steam-cook for about 2 minutes.

Stir in the spiced beancurd, garlic chives and chilli, and stir-fry for about 30 seconds. Add the sugar and soy sauce, stir-fry for about 1 minute and serve.

Polenta with olives & basil

Polenta, a finely ground cornmeal, is especially popular in Italy. Traditional polenta takes about 30 minutes to cook, but instant polenta, which is ready in minutes, is great for busy people. A popular way to serve polenta is to top it with fresh tomato sauce and a little grated cheese. Grill it until the cheese melts.

SERVES 4

600 ml (1 pint) water

¼ teaspoon salt

150 g (5 oz) instant polenta

8 black olives, pitted and sliced

3 tablespoons finely sliced basil

2 teaspoons olive oil *or* butter

freshly ground black pepper

Preheat the oven to 220°C/450°F/Gas Mark 7.

Line a small roasting tray with oven paper.

Bring the salted water to the boil. Slowly pour in the polenta, lower the heat and stir until the polenta is well mixed and has thickened. Stir in the olives, basil and half the oil. Season with pepper.

Pour the polenta into a roasting tray and spread it out to a thickness of about 2 cm (¾ in). It does not matter if the base of the tray is not fully covered. Pour over the remaining oil and bake in a preheated oven for 5 minutes – longer if you like it dry. Serve immediately.

Couscous with vegetables

Couscous is a coarse wheat semolina that is a staple of North African cuisine.
It is really like pasta, and usually comes in packets already partly cooked. The cooking
instructions usually say to add the couscous to hot water for a few minutes, but I prefer to finish
the cooking by steaming as it gives a lighter, fluffier grain. Harissa is a hot chilli paste available
from good delis and food stores. This preparation is beautifully spicy.

SERVES 4

2 medium carrots, peeled and
  halved crosswise

2 turnips, peeled and halved

1 red pepper, quartered and seeded

2 courgettes, halved crosswise

3 tomatoes, quartered

1 tablespoon tomato pureé

1 teaspoon harissa *or* chilli paste

1 teaspoon ground cumin

1 clove garlic, crushed

1 tablespoon olive oil

salt and freshly ground black pepper

400 g (14 oz) can
  chickpeas, drained

2–3 Swiss chard leaves *or* a handful
  of spinach, shredded

300 g (11 oz) couscous

a few sprigs of coriander

In a large saucepan place the carrots, turnips, pepper, courgettes, tomatoes, tomato pureé, harissa, cumin, garlic, and olive oil. Cover with water and season with salt and pepper. Bring to the boil and cook for 10 minutes.

Add the drained chickpeas and Swiss chard leaves or spinach, and cook for a further 10 minutes.

Place the couscous in a fine-mesh strainer and run cold water over it for a few minutes. Place a damp towel or muslin over the perforated compartment of your steamer and put the wet couscous over the cloth. Bring some water in the steamer base to the boil, and steam the couscous, uncovered, for 10–15 minutes or until the grains are soft. Stir with a fork to separate the grains.

Place the couscous on a dish and the vegetables and liquid separately in a serving bowl. Garnish with sprigs of coriander. Serve from the centre of the table for all to help themselves.

Tomato & spicy bean tartlets on filo

To save time, cook the base of these tartlets several hours before your meal. Other vegetables such as mushrooms or peppers can be used in place of the tomato. Borlotti beans are ideal for this dish.

SERVES 6

4 sheets filo pastry

3 tablespoons olive oil

125 ml (4 fl oz) Italian-style tomato sauce, bottled or home-made (p. 210)

3 black olives, pitted and chopped

salt and freshly ground black pepper

115 g (4 oz) cooked beans, drained

¼ teaspoon ground cumin

¼ teaspoon chilli paste

1 tablespoon coriander leaves, finely sliced

3 plum tomatoes, finely sliced

2 small courgettes, finely sliced

Preheat the oven to 180°C/350°F/Gas Mark 4.

Line a greased baking sheet with one sheet of filo pastry. Brush the pastry with a little oil and place a second pastry sheet on top. Do likewise with the third and fourth pastry sheets, brushing each layer with oil. Cut the pastry into 6 equal rectangles.

In a small bowl, mix the tomato sauce with the olives and a little pepper. Thinly spread a little of this tomato preparation in the centre of each pastry rectangle, leaving an edge of about 1 cm (⅓ in). Bake the pastry in the preheated oven until the base of the pastry is lightly browned. This takes about 10–15 minutes.

Blend the cooked beans to a purée with 1 tablespoon of the olive oil, the cumin and chilli paste. Season to taste. Spread this bean paste over the cooked pastry, sprinkle with coriander and top with the tomato and courgette slices in an attractive overlapping pattern. Place the tartlets in the preheated oven for about 10 minutes until the tomato is hot and soft. Serve immediately.

pasta, noo

These foods are currently enjoying great popularity and it is a good thing for they provide us with long-lasting energy and are low in fat. Hence we often hear of sportspeople eating a dish of pasta before a performance. These foods are also among the easiest and most popular for children to learn to cook. A bowl of plain pasta, noodles and rice, however, is not a meal in itself, and it is important to serve vegetables and a form of protein with it. Avoid eating pasta with sauces high in fat, such as those containing butter, cream, cheese or oil, and remember that pasta goes equally well with fresh herbs, tomato sauce, fish and vegetables.

dles & RICe

Always cook pasta in a large quantity of lightly salted boiling water. Read the cooking instructions on the pack or ask the people you buy fresh pasta from about cooking times.

Many varieties of noodles are available fresh or dried from Asian foodstores. Most dried noodles need only a few minutes cooking in boiling water. Fresh noodles and some thinner dried noodles need only be reheated or soaked in hot water for 2 minutes. I have provided instructions on how to cook rice in this section, or you may follow the instructions on the pack.

RICE

Pasta.

This is the basic technique for cooking pasta. The cooking time for fresh or dry pasta varies from one brand to another so you need to read the packet instructions or ask the pasta seller for advice. If serving pasta as an accompaniment, season it with a little olive oil or butter and add grated parmesan.

SERVES 2 AS A MAIN COURSE

¼ teaspoon salt

3 litres (5 pints) water

1 teaspoon olive oil (optional)

200 g (7 oz) dry pasta *or* 250 g
(9 oz) fresh pasta

In a large pot, bring the salted cold water to the boil. When boiling, add the oil and pasta, and return to the boil. Stir occasionally to prevent the pasta from sticking. Fresh pasta takes 2–5 minutes, while dry pasta takes 8–12 minutes.

Test the pasta by taking a piece with a pair of tongs. Cool briefly under the tap and bite into it. The pasta should be just a little firm in the centre – the Italians call this 'al dente'.

Once cooked, add about a cup of cold water to pasta and drain it in a colander, shaking out any excess water. Season with your favourite sauce or herb, and serve immediately.

Penne with mexican bean sauce

Penne is a cylindrical pasta that is very popular in Italy and all over the world. This dish is a main course and I like to serve it with a green salad.

SERVES 4

400 g (14 oz) penne

salt and freshly ground black pepper

1 tablespoon olive oil

½ onion, finely chopped

½ teaspoon cumin seeds

½ small chilli, finely sliced

350 ml (12 fl oz) Italian-style tomato sauce, bottled *or* home-made (p. 210)

400 g (14 oz) can cannellini beans *or* other beans of your choice

a few sprigs of coriander *or* parsley, finely chopped (optional)

Cook the penne in a large pot of salted boiling water until al dente. This usually takes between 9–11 minutes. Drain.

Meanwhile, heat half of the oil in a non-stick pan. Add the onion and cook for 4 minutes over low heat. Add the cumin seeds and chilli, and stir-fry for 1 minute. Add the tomato sauce and drained beans and bring to a simmer.

Toss the drained penne with the bean sauce. Season with salt and pepper and stir in the remaining oil. Sprinkle with coriander or parsley before serving.

Macaroni with tuna & vegetables

This is one of those family dishes where you can use up any remaining vegetables you have in the fridge.

SERVES 2

about 200 g (7 oz) macaroni

225 g (8 oz) broccoli, cut into small florets

½ teaspoon olive oil

6 mushrooms, sliced

2 tomatoes, diced

½ clove garlic, finely chopped

1 tablespoon finely sliced basil

200 g (7 oz) can of tuna in oil, drained and flaked

freshly ground black pepper

Bring a pot of lightly salted water to the boil and cook the macaroni in boiling water until al dente.

Place the broccoli in a bowl and cover with boiling water from the kettle. Drain after 2 minutes.

Heat the oil in a non-stick saucepan and cook the mushrooms for 2 minutes. Add the broccoli and stir gently. Add the tomatoes, cover and cook for about 3 minutes.

Mix the drained pasta with the vegetables, garlic, basil and tuna, and season with black pepper. Serve while hot.

Farfelle pasta with pumpkin & pine nuts

You can use another type of pasta in this dish if you wish. Try serving it with a green salad. Toast the pinenuts carefully under the grill until they just begin to brown.

SERVES 2

200 g (7 oz) pumpkin flesh, cut into small pieces

about 200 g (7 oz) farfelle pasta

salt and freshly ground black pepper

2 teaspoons olive oil

½ clove garlic, finely chopped

3 tablespoons chopped parsley

1 tablespoon pinenuts, toasted

1 tablespoon freshly grated parmesan

Place the pumpkin in a saucepan with a little water, cover and steam the pumpkin until soft. Alternatively, microwave until cooked.

Meanwhile, cook the pasta in a large volume of lightly salted boiling water.

Mash the cooked pumpkin and stir in the olive oil, garlic, parsley and a little salt and pepper to taste.

Gently toss the drained pasta with the pumpkin purée and serve sprinkled with pinenuts and grated parmesan.

Ravioli with spinach & olives

Many pasta shops make beautiful ravioli as well as other pasta parcels, like agnolotti. They are filled with meat, spinach and ricotta, mushrooms, pumpkin – the choice is wide. Read the packet instructions carefully for cooking times or ask your shopkeeper for advice.

SERVES 2

3 litres (5 pints) water

salt and freshly ground black pepper

350 g (12 oz) fresh ravioli *or*
 300 g (11 oz) dry ravioli

200 g (7 oz) young spinach leaves

1 tomato, diced

2 teaspoons olive oil

4 olives, pitted and finely sliced

1 tablespoon parmesan shavings or
 grated parmesan

If necessary, separate ravioli squares from one another. Bring the salted water to the boil. Add the pasta and stir gently. Cook the pasta until soft. Fresh ravioli takes 5–10 minutes, depending on the type used, while dry ravioli takes 10–18 minutes. Drain.

Cook the spinach in a covered saucepan until soft. (It cooks in its own steam.) Drain and season with a little salt and pepper.

Place the spinach on plates and divide the ravioli between them. Scatter over the diced tomato and drizzle the oil over the ravioli. Season with salt and pepper, top with olives and shavings of parmesan, and serve.

Spaghetti with chicken & aubergine

Be creative with this dish, and add vegetables and herbs of your choice.
Make sure the chicken and vegetables are ready before the spaghetti.

SERVES 2

2 teaspoons olive oil

1 large chicken fillet, skinned
and finely sliced

1 medium aubergine, diced

about 150 g (3½ oz) spaghetti

salt and freshly ground black pepper

about 100 g (3½ oz) baby spinach leaves

1 tomato, diced

1 clove garlic, finely chopped

1 tablespoon finely sliced basil or parsley

3 tablespoons grated parmesan

Heat half of the oil in a non-stick pan and brown the
chicken pieces for 1 minute. Transfer to a plate.

Add the remaining oil to the pan and, on high heat,
cook the aubergine until soft.

In the meantime, cook the spaghetti in a large quantity
of salted boiling water.

When the aubergine is soft, add the spinach and cook
until it has softened also. Stir in the tomato, garlic and
basil or parsley, and season with salt and pepper.

Toss the drained spaghetti with the vegetables and serve
sprinkled with a little grated parmesan.

Bolognese sauce

The vegetables in this sauce impart lots of flavour to the dish. Use very fresh mince.
The secret of a good bolognese is long slow cooking, and ideally it should cook for 2 hours.
Of course, you can reduce the cooking time if you're in a hurry but the sauce won't be as
flavoursome. The sauce will keep in the fridge for 2 to 3 days or frozen in a freezer
bag or air-tight container for up to 2 months.

SERVES 4

1 tablespoon olive oil

1 lean rasher bacon, diced

2 teaspoons chopped fresh thyme

1 small onion, peeled and finely diced

1 medium carrot, peeled and finely diced

2 sticks celery, peeled and finely diced

300 g (11 oz) lean ground beef

1 tablespoon plain flour

1 tablespoon plain tomato pureé

125 ml (4 fl oz) red wine

2 cloves garlic, crushed

500 ml (18 fl oz) Italian-style tomato sauce,
   bottled or home-made (p. 210)

salt and freshly ground black pepper

Heat the oil in a saucepan and on medium heat fry
the bacon, thyme, onion, carrot and celery for about
5 minutes. Increase the heat and add the meat to pan.
Cook for a few minutes, stirring occasionally. Stir in the
flour and tomato paste. Stir in the wine and bring to the
boil. Add the garlic and tomato sauce. Season and stir
well. Lower the heat and bring to a simmer.

Cover and cook slowly for 1–2 hours. Stir occasionally
to prevent burning or sticking, and add a little boiling
water if you feel the sauce becoming too thick at any
stage. Alternatively, you can cook the sauce in a covered
casserole dish in the oven at 150°C/300°F/Gas Mark 2
for about 1–2 hours.

Serve with your favourite pasta cooked al dente.

Chinese egg noodles with vegetables

Prepare this dish using your favourite vegetables. Broccoli, cabbage and spinach work especially well. The Chinese egg noodles (chow-mein noodles) are readily available from Asian foodstores.

SERVES 2

3 sprigs of Chinese broccoli, cut diagonally into 4 cm (about 1¾ in) pieces

200 g (7 oz) Chinese egg noodles

2 teaspoons groundnut oil

1 slice ginger, left whole

½ clove garlic, crushed

1 rasher lean bacon, finely sliced (optional)

100 g (3½ oz) bean sprouts

2 teaspoons low-salt soy sauce

about 6 cherry tomatoes, quartered

½ small red chilli, finely sliced (optional)

2 spring onions, chopped

Place the Chinese broccoli in a bowl and cover with boiling water. Drain after 4 minutes.

Place the noodles in a bowl and cover with boiling water. Drain after 3 minutes.

Heat a wok and, when hot, add the oil. Stir in the ginger, garlic and bacon, and fry for 10 seconds. Add the Chinese broccoli and stir-fry for about 2 minutes. Add the bean sprouts and stir-fry for 1 minute. Add the drained noodles, soy sauce, cherry tomatoes and chilli. Stir gently to mix well. When heated through, serve sprinkled with spring onions.

Indonesian stir-fry vegetables with mince & noodles

This is one of the first dishes my wife, Angie, cooked for
me almost twenty years ago. It is now a family favourite.

SERVES 4

150 g (5 oz) dry Asian
   noodles *or* spaghetti

1 egg

3 tablespoons water

1 tablespoon groundnut oil

½ onion, diced

1 rasher lean bacon, trimmed
   and diced

1 clove garlic, chopped

150 g (5 oz) lean minced meat

3 sticks celery, diced

½ pepper, seeded and diced

4 small carrots, diced

⅛ cabbage, shredded

½ teaspoon chilli sauce or to taste

2 teaspoons soy sauce

freshly ground black pepper

Cook the noodles for 3 minutes in boiling water. Strain
and refresh under cold running water. Drain. If using
spaghetti, cook according to the intructions on the
packet.

Beat the egg with the water. Brush a small non-stick
frying pan with oil and quickly scramble the egg.
Transfer to a plate.

Pour half of the remaining oil in a hot wok and, when
the oil is hot, fry the onion on high heat until just brown
around the edges. Transfer to a bowl, and fry the bacon
until crisp. Place with the onion.

Add the garlic to the wok and stir in the mince. Fry until
the meat is browned, stirring to remove any lumps, then
transfer to a bowl.

Heat the remaining oil in a wok and add the celery,
pepper, carrots and cabbage. Stir-fry until the
vegetables soften. If the mixture starts to burn, pour
a few tablespoons of water down the side of the wok.

Return the onion, bacon, egg, meat, and noodles to the
wok. Season with chilli, soy sauce and pepper. Toss well
to heat through and distribute the flavours. Serve.

Singapore-style noodles

Young men seem to love this dish. You will need to buy some Chinese roast pork (*char siew*), which is sold in strips by weight in some Chinese take-away shops.

SERVES 2

100 g (3½ oz) fresh Chinese
   egg noodles

1 tablespoon oil

1 teaspoon grated ginger

1 clove garlic, chopped

1 teaspoon curry powder

1 stick celery, finely sliced

1 baby carrot, finely sliced

3 tablespoons water

55 g (2 oz) cooked shrimps

100 g (3½ oz) Chinese roast
   pork, finely sliced

115 g (4 oz) bean sprouts

1 hard-boiled egg, sliced

2 spring onions, finely sliced

1 tablespoon soy sauce

a few sprigs of coriander

Place the noodles in a bowl and cover with boiling water from the kettle. Drain after 2 minutes.

Heat the oil in a wok and stir-fry the ginger, garlic, curry powder, celery and carrot for about 1 minute. Add the water down the side of the wok to stop any scorching and stir-fry for a further minute. Add the shrimps and pork and stir-fry for about 30 seconds. Add the bean sprouts and stir-fry for 30 seconds. Gently toss in the noodles, egg and spring onions. Season with soy sauce and serve sprinkled with sprigs of coriander.

Stir-fried beef & broccoli with thin noodles

Here is a simple stir-fry dish for those who love Chinese food. Once you have mastered the technique of stir-frying, try adding other vegetables to vary the dish.

SERVES 2

2 teaspoons shaoshing (Chinese rice wine) *or* dry sherry

1 teaspoon cornflour

freshly ground black pepper

2 teaspoons cold water

200 g (7 oz) lean rump steak, cut across the grain into ½ cm (¼ in) slices

200 g (7 oz) broccoli, cut into florets

200 g (7 oz) thin, fresh egg noodles

1 tablespoon groundnut oil

1 clove garlic, finely sliced

1 teaspoon grated ginger

2 teaspoons low-salt soy sauce

½ teaspoon sesame oil

In a medium bowl combine the wine, cornflour, pepper and water. Stir in the beef.

Place the broccoli in a bowl and pour over boiling water from the kettle. Drain after 2 minutes.

Place the egg noodles in a bowl and pour over boiling water from the kettle. Drain after 2 minutes.

Pour half of the groundnut oil into a hot wok and when the oil is hot, stir-fry the broccoli for about 2 minutes until tender. Transfer the broccoli to a bowl.

Heat the remaining oil and stir in the garlic and ginger. Add the beef and stir-fry on high heat for about 20–30 seconds until it changes colour. Stir in the soy sauce, sesame oil, broccoli and noodles and heat through before serving.

Steamed Rice

Rice is popular with most people and is an excellent food for
people with wheat allergies. I use a long-grain rice such as basmati or jasmine.
It's essential to cook the rice in a saucepan with a tight-fitting lid.

SERVES 3

1 cup long-grain rice

1 ½ cups cold water

a pinch of salt

1 teaspoon groundnut *or* olive oil

Rinse the rice under running water and drain.

Place the water, salt and oil in a saucepan. Add the rice, bring to a simmer and cover the pan immediately with a tight-fitting lid. Cook on low heat for 17 minutes. The rice is now ready.

For brown rice, use 1 cup brown rice to 2 cups water and cook for about 40 minutes following the above method.

Risotto with chicken & vegetables

Cooked chicken meat from a leftover roast or boiled chicken is ideal for this dish.

SERVES 3

1 tablespoon olive oil

½ onion, finely chopped

½ carrot, finely chopped

10 cm (4 in) stick celery,
   finely chopped

750 ml (1¼ pints) chicken stock (p. 204)

175 g (6 oz) risotto rice (short, round grain)

8 mushrooms, finely chopped

50 ml (2 fl oz) dry white wine

225 g (8 oz) diced, cooked chicken meat

3 tablespoons freshly grated parmesan

salt and freshly ground black pepper

1 tablespoon chopped parsley

Heat the oil in a medium saucepan and gently fry the onion, carrot and celery for about 3 minutes.

Bring the chicken stock to the boil, then reduce the heat to keep it simmering while making the risotto.

Add the rice to the vegetables and mix well for about 1 minute. Stir in the mushrooms. Add the wine and about a third of the stock to the pan and bring to a gentle simmer, stirring all the time. Simmer until almost all the stock has been absorbed, then add a little more stock. Keep adding the stock, a little at a time, stirring all the time, until the rice is cooked but still firm in the centre. You may either have a little stock left over or you may have run out, in which case add some boiling water.

Add the diced chicken to the pan 2 minutes before the rice is ready. While stirring, add the parmesan and season with salt and pepper. Taste a few grains of rice to check if it is cooked. At this point, the preparation will be creamy but not runny. Cover the risotto with a lid and rest it for about 3 minutes before serving. In all, the cooking takes about 18–20 minutes.

Sprinkle with parsley just before serving.

Paella

This Spanish dish is popular with people from the Mediterranean region who see it as a complete family meal, served with plenty of rice and vegetables and just a little meat or seafood to flavour the dish. It is a treat and a great party dish to serve from the centre of the table.

SERVES 6–8

1 tablespoon olive oil

8 small drumsticks *or* other chicken pieces, fat and skin removed

1 small onion, diced

1 red pepper, sliced

2 tomatoes, chopped

175 g (6 oz) shelled peas

225 g (8 oz) short-grain rice

750 ml (1 1/4 pints) cold water *or* chicken stock (p. 204)

salt and freshly ground black pepper

2 pinches of saffron

1/2 hot chilli

12 mussels, washed and de-bearded

125 ml (1/4 pint) dry white wine

about 8 (or more) prawns

3 tablespoons chopped parsley

Heat the oil in a wide pan or casserole dish, and brown the chicken pieces. Add the onion and stir for 2 minutes. Then add the pepper, tomatoes, peas, rice and water or stock. Bring to a simmer, season with salt, pepper, saffron and chilli. Stir gently to combine the spices. Cover and simmer for about 20 minutes.

Place the washed mussels and white wine in a pan and bring to the boil. Cover and cook for a few minutes until the mussel shells have opened.

Add the prawns to the rice and chicken mixture and cook for a further 5 minutes. Add a little extra water or strained mussel juice to the rice towards the end of the cooking if it becomes too dry.

Serve the paella in the pan or dish it was cooked in, with the opened mussels on top. Sprinkle with the parsley and serve.

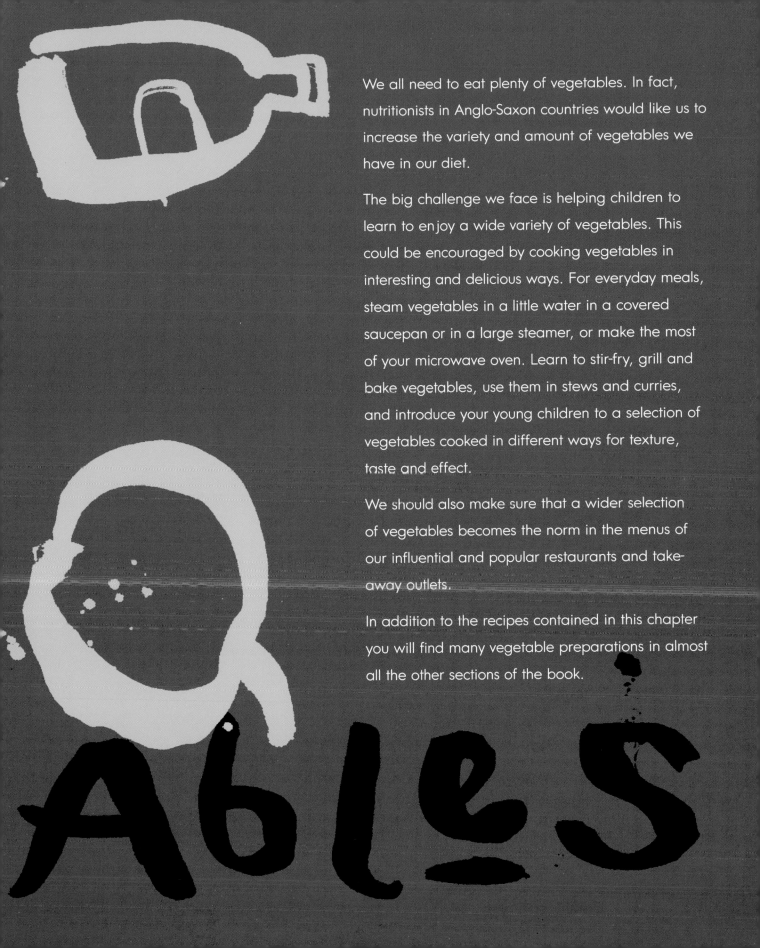

We all need to eat plenty of vegetables. In fact, nutritionists in Anglo-Saxon countries would like us to increase the variety and amount of vegetables we have in our diet.

The big challenge we face is helping children to learn to enjoy a wide variety of vegetables. This could be encouraged by cooking vegetables in interesting and delicious ways. For everyday meals, steam vegetables in a little water in a covered saucepan or in a large steamer, or make the most of your microwave oven. Learn to stir-fry, grill and bake vegetables, use them in stews and curries, and introduce your young children to a selection of vegetables cooked in different ways for texture, taste and effect.

We should also make sure that a wider selection of vegetables becomes the norm in the menus of our influential and popular restaurants and take-away outlets.

In addition to the recipes contained in this chapter you will find many vegetable preparations in almost all the other sections of the book.

AbleS

Mashed potato

The secret to perfect mashed potato is
to use a food mill (mouli) to purée the potato.

SERVES 2

3 medium potatoes, peeled
   and quartered

salt and freshly ground
   black pepper

125 ml (4 fl oz) milk

1 teaspoon butter *or* olive oil

Place the potatoes in a saucepan and cover with
cold water. Season with a little salt, bring to the
boil and cook for 10–15 minutes until the potatoes
are just soft. Drain.

Heat the milk in a small saucepan.

Pass the potato through the food mill and return
potato to the saucepan. Alternatively, mash the
potato with a vegetable masher. Using a wooden
spoon, stir the hot milk into the potato and mix
until very smooth. Stir in the butter or oil, season
with salt and pepper and serve.

Roast Potato wedges

These easy-to-make potato wedges are
satisfying and delicious. Line the roasting tray
with baking paper to prevent sticking.

SERVES 4

4 medium potatoes

1 teaspoon sweet paprika

a pinch of cayenne pepper

1/2 teaspoon salt

2 sprigs of thyme, chopped

freshly ground black pepper

1 tablespoon olive oil

Wash the potatoes and halve lengthwise. Cut each
half into 4–6 long wedges. Place in a saucepan,
cover with cold water and bring to the boil. Boil
potatoes for 1 minute then drain.

Preheat the oven to 240°C/475°F/Gas Mark 9.

In a medium bowl combine the paprika, cayenne
pepper, salt, thyme and about 1/2 teaspoon freshly
ground pepper. Gently toss the drained potato
wedges with the spices. Add the oil and toss
gently to coat the potatoes. Place the wedges on
a shallow roasting tray lined with baking paper
and roast in a preheated oven for about
20 minutes or until cooked and golden.

Roast vegetables

Most people love roast vegetables with
roast meat. Cook the vegetables in a separate tray so they do not absorb the fat from the
meat. Start roasting your vegetables in the
top part of the oven about 10 minutes after you start cooking the meat.

SERVES 8

4 medium carrots, peeled and cut
   into 3–4 cm (1–1 ½ in) pieces

about 400 g (14 oz) pumpkin, peeled
   and cut into bite-sized pieces

8 small potatoes, peeled

3 tablespoons olive oil

½ teaspoon paprika

salt and freshly ground black pepper

Preheat the oven to 180°C/350°F/Gas Mark 4.

Place the vegetables in a saucepan with enough cold
water to cover and bring to the boil. Allow to boil for
2 minutes. Drain well and place in a bowl with the olive
oil, paprika and salt and pepper. Toss well.

Line a flat roasting tray with oven paper and place
the vegetables on the tray. Bake for 30–40 minutes
until cooked, turning 2 or 3 times during the cooking.
Serve hot.

Vegetables with red pepper sauce

Indulge yourself with this dish and choose your favourite seasonal vegetables.
In this recipe I steam all the vegetables, except for the potatoes, which are boiled
in their skin. Save time by making the pepper sauce the day before.

SERVES 2

1 cup red pepper sauce (p. 213)

100 g (3½ oz) cabbage

6 baby carrots, peeled

1 small leek, sliced diagonally into
   3 cm (1½ in) pieces

1 corn cob, cut into 3 cm (1½ in)
   lengths

about 4 asparagus spears,
   cut diagonally into 5 cm
   (2 in) lengths

2 small potatoes, boiled

1 tablespoon finely snipped chives

salt and freshly ground black pepper

Trim away any hard ribs on the cabbage leaves. Bring water to the boil in a steamer. Place the carrots, leek and cabbage in the steamer and cook for 4 minutes. Add the corn and asparagus, and cook until the vegetables are just soft, about 5–10 minutes.

Sprinkle the chives over the vegetables and season with salt and pepper. Serve with either hot or cold red pepper sauce.

Cauliflower with light cheese sauce

Cauliflower with cheese sauce is one of the most popular vegetable dishes. The traditional method is a little rich so try this lighter version and make it a few times before making your final judgment.

SERVES 2

about 300 g (11 oz) very white
  cauliflower, left whole

250 ml (9 fl oz) skimmed milk

½ onion, sliced

salt and freshly ground black pepper

1 tablespoon cornflour

1 tablespoon cold water

2 pinches of grated nutmeg

a pinch of cayenne pepper

¼ teaspoon sweet paprika

4 tablespoons grated cheese such
  as Swiss-style or mozzarella

Bring water to the boil in a vegetable steamer and steam the cauliflower until just soft.

Bring the milk to the boil with the onion and a little salt and pepper.

In a small bowl mix the cornflour with water. Add the mixture to the simmering milk and stir for about 5 minutes. Strain into a bowl. Stir the nutmeg and cayenne pepper into the sauce.

Preheat the oven grill.

Place the cauliflower into an oven dish. Spoon over the sauce and sprinkle the paprika and cheese on top. Place under a hot grill and cook until lightly browned on top.

Mixed vegetable stir-fry

You'll get better at preparing this dish each time you do it. Remember to cook the vegetables in order from the hardest to the softest, for example, the pepper before the mushrooms.

SERVES 3–4

about 150 g (5 oz) green beans, cut diagonally into 3 cm (1½ in) lengths

about 1 tablespoon groundnut oil

1 clove garlic, crushed

3 thin slices fresh ginger, left whole

1 red pepper, halved, seeded, and finely sliced

about 100 g (3½ oz) fresh shiitake mushrooms, halved

about 100 g (3½ oz) bean sprouts, rinsed

about 100 g (3½ oz) fresh or canned baby corn cobs

½ teaspoon sugar

¼ teaspoon sesame oil

1 tablespoon soy sauce (optional)

¼ teaspoon chilli paste (optional)

Place the beans in a bowl and cover with boiling water from the kettle. Drain after 3 minutes.

Heat a wok, and when hot, add the oil. Stir in the garlic and ginger, add the beans and stir-fry for 30 seconds. Add the pepper and toss for 30 seconds, then add the mushrooms, bean sprouts and corn cobs and stir-fry for a few minutes until the vegetables are soft. Stir in the sugar and sesame oil and mix well. Add the soy sauce and chilli paste, and serve.

chef's note

If the vegetables start to scorch during cooking, pour 3 tablespoons of cold water down the side of the wok to create steam and prevent any sticking or burning.

Cauliflower & mushroom curry

Cauliflower absorbs the flavour of spices in a very agreeable way. Use broccoli instead, if you wish, but reduce the cooking time.

SERVES 2

2 teaspoons groundnut oil

½ onion, chopped

1 teaspoon grated ginger

1 teaspoon curry powder

250 ml (9fl oz) Italian-style tomato sauce, bottled *or* home-made (p. 210)

300 g (11 oz) cauliflower, cut into florets

100 g (3½ oz) mushrooms, quartered

salt and freshly ground black pepper

1 tablespoon sultanas

juice of ¼ lemon

1 tablespoon finely sliced coriander *or* parsley leaves

Heat the oil in a non-stick saucepan and on low heat fry the onion and ginger for about 3 minutes. Stir in the curry powder, then the tomato sauce, cauliflower and mushrooms. Season with a little salt and pepper and bring to a simmer.

Add the sultanas, cover and cook for about 5 minutes, stirring occasionally. Stir in the lemon juice and sprinkle with coriander or parsley before serving.

Stir-fried baby bok choy & abalone mushrooms

You can replace the bok choy with spinach or Chinese broccoli. Abalone mushrooms can be found in most Asian foodstores and supermarkets.

SERVES 2

3 heads baby bok choy (a bunch is often made up of 3 heads)

1 tablespoon groundnut oil

1 clove garlic, sliced

a few drops sesame oil

about 150 g (5 oz) abalone mushrooms

2 teaspoons oyster sauce

1 tablespoon shaoshing wine (rice wine) *or* dry sherry

½ teaspoon sugar

Quarter the bok choy lengthwise and wash well in cold water. Place the bok choy in a bowl and cover with boiling water from the kettle. Leave for 2 minutes. Drain.

Pour half the groundnut oil into a hot wok. Add the garlic and bok choy, and stir-fry for 1 minute. Add the sesame oil and toss through to distribute the flavours. Transfer the bok choy to a serving dish and keep warm.

Return wok to the heat. Add the remaining oil and stir-fry the mushrooms for about 20 seconds. Add the oyster sauce, rice wine and sugar and stir well. Spoon the mushrooms and sauce over the bok choy and serve hot.

Chinese broccoli with oyster sauce

I really love Chinese broccoli, and this simple dish is wonderful either with grilled or pan-fried fish or chicken, or even with noodles.

SERVES 3

about 400 g (14 oz) Chinese broccoli

1 tablespoon groundnut oil

1 tablespoon oyster sauce

½ teaspoon sugar

Wash the Chinese broccoli and cut the long stalks in half.

Bring a medium saucepan of water to the boil. Add the oil and broccoli, and after the water has returned to the boil, cook broccoli for 1 minute. Drain, reserving a little of the cooking liquid, and transfer the broccoli to a serving dish.

In a small bowl mix together the oyster sauce, sugar and 1 tablespoon of the cooking liquid from the broccoli. Pour this over the Chinese broccoli and serve immediately.

Ratatouille

This flavoursome vegetable dish can be served with fish, meat, pasta and eggs, and is even delicious cold.

SERVES 3

1 tablespoon olive oil

½ onion, diced

2 sprigs of thyme or parsley or 4 basil leaves

2 cloves garlic, chopped

½ red pepper, cut into 2 cm (¾ in) pieces

2 medium courgettes, cut into 2 cm (¾ in) pieces

1 small aubergine, cut into 2 cm (¾ in) pieces

3 tomatoes, diced

salt and freshly ground black pepper

Heat the oil in a non-stick saucepan and stir-fry the onion and thyme for about 2 minutes on medium heat.

Add the garlic and pepper and stir-fry for another 2 minutes. Add the courgettes and aubergine and stir well for 1 minute before adding the tomatoes. Season with a little salt and pepper, cover, and cook for 10–20 minutes, depending on how well done you like the vegetables.

Artichokes Provençale

I particularly love this dish. Artichokes are a superb vegetable and the
result here is quite exotic. The most demanding part of the dish is in the preparation:
you have to trim away the leaves of the artichoke until you reach the heart.

SERVES 3–4

1 litre (2 pints) cold water

½ lemon

6 large artichokes

1 tablespoon olive oil

1 small onion, finely chopped

1 teaspoon coriander seeds

12 fennel seeds

1 teaspoon tomato pureé

½ glass dry white wine

4 medium tomatoes, chopped

3–4 sprigs of parsley, chopped

an extra 2 slices of lemon, quartered

salt and freshly ground black pepper

Pour about 1 litre (2 pints) cold water into a bowl and place the half lemon into it.

Using a very sharp knife, cut off the artichoke stalks. Cut through the top part of the artichokes, leaving about 3½ cm (about 1⅓ in) of the base. Trim away the remaining leaves, leaving only the heart. Using a spoon, scoop out the choke (the hairy part) from the centre of the heart. When all the hearts are trimmed and clean, place them in the water and rub them with the lemon to prevent discolouring.

Heat the oil in a pan and gently fry the onion for 3–4 minutes. Cut each artichoke heart into 6 pieces. Add to the pan and stir for 1 minute. Add the coriander and fennel seeds, stir in the tomato pureé, wine, and the chopped tomatoes, parsley sprigs and pieces of lemon. Season, cover the pan and cook, stirring occasionally, for about 15 minutes or until the artichokes are soft.

Serve hot or cold. I enjoy it best cold myself.

Grilled vegetables

Grilled vegetables can be cooked on a cast-iron grill or on the barbecue. They are delicious as part of an antipasto selection, as a garnish for fish or meat or as a sandwich filling.

SERVES ABOUT 4

3 tablespoons olive oil

1 teaspoon freshly chopped thyme

1 clove garlic, finely chopped (optional)

1 aubergine, cut into 1 cm (1/3 in) slices lengthwise

2 courgettes, cut into 1 cm (1/3 in) slices lengthwise

2 large mushrooms, cut into 1 cm (1/3 in) slices

1 red pepper, cut into about 8 long strips

salt and freshly ground black pepper

Mix two-thirds of the oil with the thyme and brush the vegetables on both sides. This can be done several hours in advance. Mix the remaining oil with the garlic.

Heat the grill or barbecue. Place the vegetables on the grill and cook for 1 minute. Move the vegetables a quarter of a turn to form a criss-cross pattern and cook for a further minute. Turn over and cook the second side, taking care not to burn the vegetables. Brush lightly with the garlic oil and season with a little salt and pepper before serving.

chef's note

It is important before starting to ensure that the grill or barbecue is very clean.

SEAFOOD

Much research has been done on the nutritional value of fish, and the results are always positive, especially when the fish has been cooked in little or no oil at all. While most varieties of fish are naturally low in fat, they do contain a fatty acid known as omega-3, which has been associated with helping lower blood fat, reduce blood pressure and prevent the blood from clotting too readily. My experience has taught me that men, especially those who love to go fishing, generally feel more comfortable handling fish than women do. So maybe the men could become the family fish cooks!

Fish takes little time to cook. A 3 cm (1½ in) thick fish fillet takes 5 to 6 minutes (2½ to 3 minutes per side) in a non-stick pan over medium heat. A fish cutlet takes about the same length of time. Fish fillets and cutlets can be easily cooked under the grill for about 2½ to 3 minutes on each side. Whole fish will take a little longer. Whole fish, fish fillets and cutlets can also be cooked in the oven in a baking tray. Fish retains its lovely flavour when simply steamed in a little liquid (water, stock or wine) or cooked with vegetables (tomato, mushrooms or celery). Whole fish are lovely pan-fried or baked; their cooking times depend on their shape and weight. Enjoy fish two or three times a week.

Pan-fried fish fillets with asparagus & mushrooms

Fish, mushrooms and asparagus go well together. Ask your fishmonger
for the freshest fish available.

SERVES 2

about 6–8 asparagus spears, cut
diagonally into 4 cm (1½ in) pieces

2 teaspoons olive oil

2 x 150 g (5 oz) fresh fish fillets

salt and freshly ground black pepper

200 g (7 oz) mushrooms, sliced

2 slices of lemon (garnish)

2 spring onions, finely sliced (garnish)

Bring cold water to the boil in a medium saucepan
and boil or steam the asparagus until cooked. Drain.

Heat the olive oil in a non-stick frying pan and cook
the fish, skinned side first, for 2½ minutes. Turn the fish
over and cook for about 2½ minutes on the other
side. Season with a little salt and pepper, transfer to
a plate and cover with foil to keep warm.

Add mushrooms to the pan and stir-fry until soft. Stir
in the asparagus and season to taste. Place the
vegetables around the fish. Garnish with the lemon
slices and spring onions, and serve.

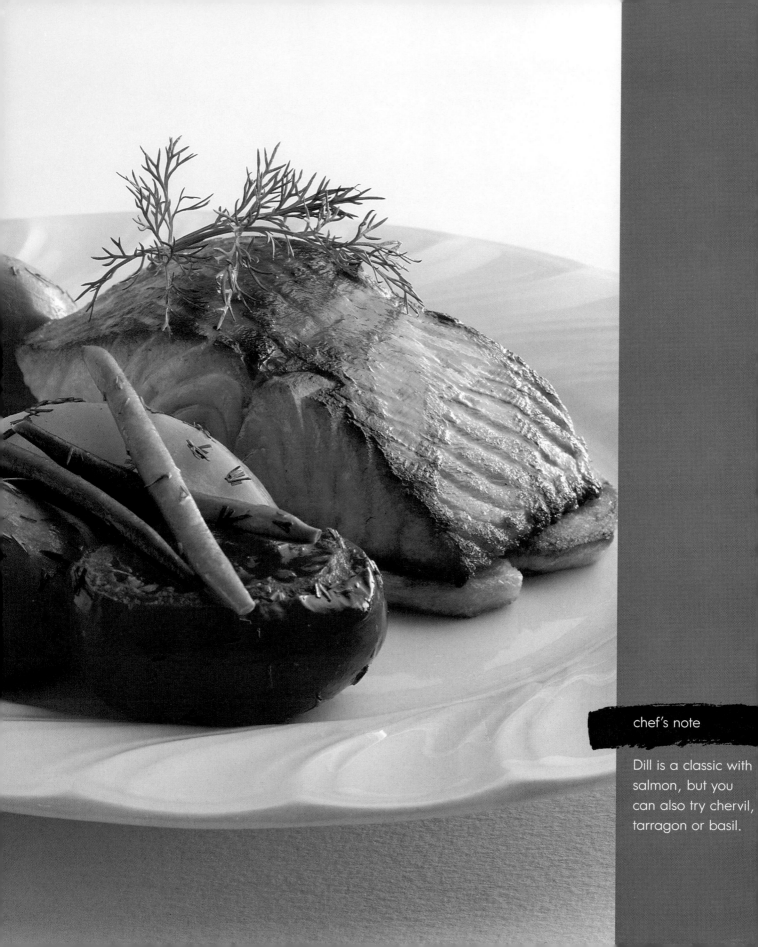

chef's note

Dill is a classic with salmon, but you can also try chervil, tarragon or basil.

Panfried Salmon with dill & vegetables .

The vegetables in this dish can be steamed or microwaved, and if you wish, serve the dish with steamed or baked potatoes. The salmon can be replaced by another fish of your choice.

SERVES 2

4 baby carrots, peeled

1 small swede *or* turnip, peeled and quartered

100 g (3½ oz) beans, topped and tailed

1 tablespoon olive oil

2 x 120 g (4 oz) salmon fillets, skin on or off

1 tomato, halved

salt and freshly ground black pepper

3 sprigs of dill, 1 sprig chopped and the others left whole

2 lemon wedges

Bring water to the boil in a steamer. Add the carrots and swede, cover and cook for 4 minutes. Add the beans and steam until just cooked.

Heat half the oil in a non-stick pan and pan-fry the salmon and tomato halves for about 2½–3 minutes on each side. Season with a little salt and pepper.

Toss the steamed vegetables with the remaining olive oil and chopped dill, and season with pepper.

Sprinkle the lemon juice over the fish and serve with the vegetables and the sprig of dill.

Fish fillet with tomato & olives in foil

Serve this easy dish with steamed or microwaved broccoli or French beans, or with a green salad. Ask your fishmonger for the freshest fish fillets available. You will need a 30 cm (12 in) square of foil.

SERVES 1

a little olive oil

1 small tomato, cut into 1 cm (1/3 in) slices

a sprig of parsley *or* about 4 basil leaves

150 g (5 oz) fish fillet

freshly ground black pepper

2 black olives, pitted and finely sliced

1 lemon wedge

Preheat the oven to 200°C/400°F/ Gas Mark 6.

Brush the centre of the foil with a little olive oil.

Place half the tomato slices in the centre of the foil and place the parsley and fish fillet on top. Season with a little pepper and top with olives and the remaining tomato slices. Squeeze a few drops of lemon juice over the fish and close the foil to seal the contents. Place on a tray in the preheated oven and cook for about 10 minutes.

To serve, carefully open the fish parcel (the steam escaping from the foil can burn) and transfer the contents to a plate. Spoon over the cooking juices and accompany with vegetables of your choice.

John dory with chinese broccoli

John Dory is a superb firm fish, easy to handle and cook. It is not usually available in the supermarket – you may need to order it from a reliable fishmonger.

SERVES 2

about 400 g (14 oz) Chinese broccoli

1 teaspoon groundnut oil

2 x 150 g (5 oz) John Dory fillets, skinned

2 teaspoons low-salt soy sauce

juice of 1/4 lemon

2 spring onions, cut into 1 cm (1/3 in) pieces

freshly ground black pepper (optional)

Trim away the hard broccoli stalks and wash well. Bring a saucepan of cold water to the boil and cook the broccoli for 3 minutes. Drain.

Heat the oil in a non-stick frying pan. Cook the fish for 2½ minutes, turn, and cook the other side for 2½ minutes. Transfer the fillets to a serving plate.

Add soy sauce and lemon juice to the pan. Toss in the spring onions and broccoli, and stir to distribute the flavours.

Place the broccoli around the fish and spoon over the sauce. Season with black pepper and serve.

Trout with Almonds

To prepare this delicate dish use a large, preferably non-stick, frying pan that will hold the trout comfortably. Otherwise, cook the fish on the barbecue or under the grill. I like to eat the fish first on its own followed by a separate salad or vegetable. It makes an ideal Sunday lunch.

SERVES 2

1 tablespoon flaked almonds

2 small trout, scaled

a little plain flour

salt and freshly ground black pepper

3 tablespoons olive oil

3 tablespoons chopped parsley

juice of ½ lemon

Lightly brown the almonds under the grill or in a hot oven. Watch them carefully – they burn very quickly.

Briefly rinse the scaled trout under cold running water and pat dry with kitchen paper. Place the flour on a plate and season with salt and pepper. Coat the fish lightly with flour.

Heat about two-thirds of the oil in a pan. Place the trout carefully in the pan and cook for about 4 minutes on each side.

Carefully transfer the trout to serving plates and sprinkle with toasted almonds and chopped parsley. Sprinkle the fish with the remaining oil and lemon juice and serve immediately.

Marinated Sardine fillets with tomato sauce

Many fishmongers now sell sardines that have already been filleted. For this dish, buy sardines on the day you eat them as they need to be very fresh. The tomato sauce may be prepared the day before and it is best to marinate the sardines for between 2 and 6 hours.

SERVES 4

juice of 3 freshly squeezed lemons

about 12 fennel seeds *or* a pinch of aniseed

8–12 sardines, filleted

a handful of greens, such as rocket

250 ml (9 fl oz) Italian-style tomato sauce, bottled or home-made (p. 210)

1 tablespoon extra-virgin olive oil

8 coriander seeds, crushed

about 4 peppercorns, crushed

a few sprigs of fresh herbs, such as dill, parsley or chervil

Place the lemon juice and fennel seeds in a deep dish. Line the dish with sardines and shake to allow the juice to cover the fish. Refrigerate for at least 2 hours.

Drain the sardines and place on top of the greens in the centre of four large plates. Spoon the tomato sauce around the fish and drizzle over a little olive oil. Sprinkle with crushed coriander and peppercorns, and top with fresh herbs. Enjoy the dish with fresh bread.

Sardines with pumpkin & brussels sprout purée

I consider sardines a real treat and yet they are one of the least expensive fish available. It is best to buy them very fresh and eat them on the same day. Use a non-stick pan to cook the sardines.

SERVES 2

about 150 g (5 oz) brussels sprouts, trimmed and halved

about 150 g (5 oz) pumpkin, peeled and cut into 1 cm (1/3 in) thick pieces

salt and freshly ground black pepper

a pinch of cayenne pepper

2 teaspoons butter

1 tablespoon olive oil

12–14 sardines, gutted and cleaned

2 lemon wedges

Bring water to the boil in a steamer. Add the sprouts and pumpkin to the steamer and cook until soft. In either a blender or food mill, separately blend the sprouts and pumpkin to a purée and season each with a little salt, pepper, cayenne and 1 teaspoon each of butter.

Heat the oil in a non-stick frying pan and cook the sardines for 2 minutes on each side. Season with salt and pepper and serve sprinkled with lemon juice and accompanied by the puréed vegetables.

Tagliatelle marinara with vegetables

Adapt this dish to your taste by choosing your favourite seafood and pasta shape.

SERVES 2

200 g (7 oz) tagliatelle

200 g (7 oz) mangetout, topped and tailed

1 tablespoon olive oil

4 prawns, shelled and deveined

8 scallops, washed

100 g (3½ oz) firm fish fillets, cut into bite-sized pieces

½ red pepper, diced

1 tablespoon brandy (optional)

250 ml (9 fl oz) Italian-style tomato sauce, bottled or home-made (p. 210)

salt and freshly ground black pepper

a pinch of cayenne pepper

1 clove garlic, finely chopped

1 tablespoon finely shredded basil or parsley

Bring a large pot of lightly salted water to the boil and cook the pasta in boiling water until al dente.

Place the mangetout in a bowl and pour over some boiling water from the kettle. After 2 minutes, drain.

Heat the olive oil in a non-stick pan and cook the prawns, scallops and fish for about 2 minutes. Transfer to a plate. Add the pepper to the pan and stir-fry on medium heat for 2 minutes. Add the brandy and tomato sauce, and bring to the boil. Season with salt, pepper and cayenne. Mix the seafood, garlic and basil with the sauce and toss gently with the drained spaghetti and mangetout. Serve immediately.

Stir-fried fish with bean sprouts & spinach

For this easy-to-prepare dish choose the freshest firm fish you can get your hands on and, if unsure as to freshness, ask your fishmonger for help.

SERVES 2

300 g (11 oz) firm fresh fish fillets,
  cut into 1 cm (⅓ in) strips

2 teaspoons shaoshing wine (Chinese
  rice wine) *or* dry sherry

2 teaspoons cornflour

½ small egg white

1 litre (1¾ pints) cold water

2 teaspoons groundnut oil

1 slice fresh ginger

½ clove garlic, finely sliced

about 100 g (3½ oz) bean sprouts,
  washed and picked through

about 225 g (8 oz) young spinach leaves

½ teaspoon sesame oil

juice of ½ lemon

¼ teaspoon chilli paste

2 teaspoons soy sauce

Mix the fish in a bowl with the wine, cornflour and egg white. Marinate for 20 minutes in the refrigerator.

Bring the water to the boil in a wok. Drop the fish strips into the boiling water and after 30 seconds tip the fish into a colander to drain.

Reheat the wok and add the oil. When the oil is hot, stir in the ginger and garlic, then immediately (otherwise the garlic will burn) add the bean sprouts and spinach. Stir-fry until soft. Stir in the sesame oil, lemon juice, chilli paste and soy sauce. Return the fish to the wok and gently mix with the vegetables. Heat through and serve immediately.

CHiNese-style fish cutlets with spinach

Tell your fishmonger how you intend to cook the fish and allow him or her to help you choose the best and freshest fish for the task. If you wish, use a whole fish instead of cutlets.

SERVES 2

1 teaspoon groundnut oil

½ teaspoon sesame oil

1 teaspoon honey

¼ teaspoon chilli paste

½ clove garlic, finely chopped

1 teaspoon grated ginger

juice of ½ lemon

2 teaspoons low-salt soy sauce

2 x 120 g (4 oz) fish steaks

about 300 g (11 oz) young
   spinach leaves

salt and freshly ground black pepper

1 teaspoon sesame seeds

2 spring onions, finely sliced

Preheat the oven to 200°C/400°F/Gas Mark 6.

In a bowl, mix the groundnut oil, half the sesame oil, honey, chilli paste, garlic, ginger, lemon juice and soy sauce.

Place the fish cutlets in a small oven dish and pour over the marinade. Turn the fish over to coat the other side. Place the dish in the preheated oven. After 5 minutes turn the fish over, cover with foil and cook for a further 5–10 minutes.

Wash the spinach and drain well. Heat the remaining sesame oil in a non-stick pan. Add the spinach, cover with a lid and cook for 3–4 minutes until the leaves have wilted. Season.

Place the spinach on a plate and sprinkle with sesame seeds. Put the fish on top, spoon over the sauce, sprinkle with spring onions and serve.

Curried mackerel with coriander & celery

Any other firm fish may be used instead of mackerel, either whole fish or fillets. Try gurnard or red snapper if they are available. If using fillets, reduce the cooking time.
Bottled tamarind paste is available from Asian foodstores.

SERVES 2

600 g (1¼ lb) mackerel

juice of ½ lemon

1 teaspoon tamarind paste

125 ml (4 fl oz) hot water

2 cm (¾ in) piece ginger, peeled

2 cloves garlic

4 tablespoons chopped fresh coriander leaves

½ small red chilli, or to taste

3 tablespoons groundnut oil

½ small onion, chopped

¼ teaspoon cumin seeds

½ teaspoon ground cumin

1 teaspoon ground coriander

1 teaspoon turmeric

a pinch of chilli powder

freshly ground black pepper

4–5 sticks celery, peeled and cut into bite-sized pieces

Cut the fish into pieces, if you wish, and pour the lemon juice over the fish.

Dilute the tamarind paste in the hot water.

Blend the ginger, garlic, coriander leaves and red chilli to a purée.

Heat the oil in a large frying pan or wok. Add the onion and cook for about 4 minutes on low heat. Stir in the cumin seeds and cook for 1 minute before stirring in the ground cumin, coriander, turmeric, chilli powder and a little pepper. Cook for about 2 minutes. Add the ginger and coriander purée and cook for 1 minute. Add the diluted tamarind, bring to a simmer and cook for about 10 minutes.

Steam or microwave the celery until cooked.

Place the fish in the spicy sauce and shake the pan to allow the sauce to thoroughly coat the fish. Simmer for 3 minutes, turn the fish over and cook for another 3–5 minutes, depending on the thickness of the fish.

To serve, place the fish over the celery and spoon over the sauce. Serve immediately with steamed rice.

Salmon Tartlets on filo

This dish can be prepared with a fish other than salmon. Try fillets of red mullet or tuna and, if you wish, alter the seasoning to suit your taste or the occasion. Serve with a mixed green salad.

SERVES 6

4 sheets filo pastry

3 tablespoons olive oil

125 ml (4 fl oz) Italian-style tomato sauce, bottled or home-made (p. 210)

1 anchovy fillet, finely chopped

3 black olives, pitted and chopped

freshly ground black pepper

200 g (7 oz) salmon fillet, cut into 6 thin slices

a small sprig of lemon thyme, finely chopped

salt

about 6 green olives, finely chopped

a few sprigs of chervil

Preheat the oven to 180°C/350°F/Gas Mark 4.

Line a baking sheet with one sheet of filo pastry. Brush the pastry with a little oil and place a second sheet of pastry on top. Do likewise with the third and fourth pastry sheets, brushing each sheet with a little oil.

Cut out 6 rounds of pastry by placing a saucer on top of the pastry and going round the edges of the saucer with the blade of a knife. Discard pastry around circles.

In a small bowl mix the tomato sauce with 1 teaspoon of the olive oil, the anchovy and olives, and season with black pepper. Thinly spread a little of this tomato preparation in the centre of each pastry round, leaving a 1 cm (1/3 in) edge. Bake the pastry rounds in the preheated oven until done. This takes about 10–15 minutes.

Coat the salmon with the remaining olive oil and lemon thyme and season with salt and pepper. Place the salmon slices on the cooked pastry rounds. Place the tartlets in the oven for a few minutes until the salmon just starts to change colour. Serve sprinkled with chopped green olives and a few sprigs of chervil.

Spicy stir-fried prawns on bok choy

Enjoy this dish either on its own or serve it as part of a Chinese meal.
Most prawns available now have been frozen, so if you can't obtain fresh
prawns choose prawns that are still frozen or just beginning to thaw at
the time of purchase. Avoid soft-looking prawns with dark spots.

SERVES 2

12–18 prawns, shelled and deveined

1 tablespoon shaoshing wine (Chinese rice wine) *or* dry sherry

1 tablespoon cornflour

½ small egg white

2 tablespoons tomato sauce *or* ketchup

3 heads bok choy, halved

4 baby carrots, cut into small pieces

500 ml (18 fl oz) water

1 tablespoon groundnut oil

1 clove garlic, finely chopped

2 teaspoons grated ginger

1 spring onion, very finely sliced

½ small red chilli, finely sliced

In a bowl, mix the prawns with half the rice wine, cornflour and egg white. Refrigerate for 30 minutes.

In another bowl mix the remaining wine and tomato sauce.

Wash the bok choy well. Bring a large saucepan of water to the boil and cook the bok choy and carrot pieces for 2 minutes. Drain.

In a wok bring the water to the boil. Drop in the marinated prawns and cook for 30 seconds until they change colour. Tip immediately into a colander and drain.

Reheat the wok and add half the oil to the wok. When the oil is hot, stir-fry the bok choy and carrots for 2 minutes. Transfer the vegetables to serving plates and keep warm. Heat the remaining oil and stir in the garlic, ginger and spring onion, and cook gently for 2 minutes. Stir in the wine and tomato mixture and the chilli. Return the prawns to the wok to reheat and coat with the sauce. Spoon the prawns and sauce over the bed of vegetables and serve immediately.

Tuna & Fennel casserole

Fennel, a vegetable which is usually available in autumn and winter, is very popular in Mediterranean countries for its aniseed flavour. This casserole is lovely served with steamed potatoes.

SERVES 2

1 medium globe fennel

1 tablespoon olive oil

2 tomatoes, sliced

1 clove garlic, crushed

4 sprigs of parsley, chopped

300 g (11 oz) tuna cutlet

salt and freshly ground black pepper

a sprig of thyme, finely chopped

½ glass dry white wine

Preheat the oven to 200°C/400°F/Gas Mark 6.

Trim the fennel of any damaged leaves and trim the top. Cut the fennel into 1 cm (⅓ in) slices.

Place half the olive oil in an ovenproof pan. Top with half of the tomato slices, the garlic, half the parsley and the fennel. Place the fish on top and season with a little salt, pepper and thyme. Top with the remaining parsley, oil and tomato. Pour over the wine, cover with foil and a lid and bake in the preheated oven for about 30 minutes or until the fish and vegetables are soft and cooked through.

Scampi & leeks with a chive dressing

This is an entrée or light meal that those who love typically French flavours will enjoy. Leeks are a very popular vegetable in France – try to get the smallest leeks you can. If scampi are unavailable, use prawns.

SERVES 6

6 very small leeks

18 scampi

a little plain flour

salt and freshly ground black pepper

3 tablespoons olive oil

2 teaspoons raspberry vinegar

3 tablespoons snipped chives

Wash the leeks and remove any damaged leaves. Steam, microwave or boil the leeks until just cooked, then cut into about 5 cm (2 in) lengths. Place on a serving platter.

Shell and devein the scampi (you may have to use a pair of scissors for this). Coat the scampi with a little flour and season with salt and pepper.

Heat 2 teaspoons of oil in a non-stick frying pan and cook the scampi for 1 minute on both sides.

To make the dressing, mix the raspberry vinegar with the remaining olive oil, season with salt and pepper, and mix in the chives.

Serve the scampi and leeks immediately with the dressing spooned over.

Scallops, asparagus & salad

Fresh scallops are a must for this special dish. Replace the scallops with prawns if you wish. Use baby spinach, rocket or other green salad leaves of your choice.

SERVES 6

about 18 asparagus spears

200 g (7 oz) salad leaves

2 shallots, finely chopped

2 teaspoons raspberry vinegar

about 3 tablespoons olive oil

salt and freshly ground black pepper

about 30 firm scallops

12 sprigs of chervil

3 tablespoons chopped walnuts

Peel the asparagus spears and snap off the hard part at the base. Wash, then steam or microwave the asparagus until cooked.

Wash and dry the salad leaves.

In a salad bowl thoroughly combine the shallots, vinegar and 2 tablespoons olive oil, and season with salt and pepper. Toss the asparagus and salad leaves in half the dressing.

Heat the remaining oil in a non-stick pan and pan-fry the scallops on either side for about 30 seconds.

Place the salad leaves and asparagus in the centre of a serving dish. Distribute the scallops around the salad and spoon over the remaining dressing. Dot with sprigs of chervil and walnuts, and serve.

The flavour of chicken is very popular and this tender meat can be prepared in hundreds of ways, as most herbs and spices seem to go well with it. Over the last ten years, poulterers have become quite creative in the variety of cuts they produce from a chicken. Many cuts are now available with or without the skin, on the bone or deboned, whole or diced, sliced or minced. It is preferable to trim all visible fat from the chicken or chicken pieces and to cook it without the skin. Chicken pieces must be used within two days of purchase, and if unsure about freshness, smell it. Your nose will let you know. Chicken casseroles with vegetables are popular and simple to prepare, and novice cooks will be thrilled with the results. Use a minimum of fat when cooking chicken and remember that like other sources of protein, chicken should be eaten in moderation.

poultry

Asian-style barbecued chicken

Use your favourite cut of chicken for this popular barbecue dish. If you have time, marinate the meat for 2 to 6 hours. It is lovely served with a salad.

SERVES 2

½ teaspoon honey

¼ teaspoon chilli paste

2 teaspoons low-salt soy sauce

¼ teaspoon sesame oil

½ clove garlic, finely chopped

½ teaspoon grated ginger

juice of ¼ lemon

freshly ground black pepper

2 chicken thighs, skinned and
   trimmed of all visible fat

For the marinade, mix the honey with the chilli paste, soy sauce, sesame oil, garlic, ginger, lemon juice and a little black pepper in a medium-sized bowl.

Add the chicken and coat thoroughly with the marinade. Cover with foil and refrigerate until 10 minutes before cooking.

Heat a lightly oiled barbecue or grill and cook the chicken for about 15–20 minutes, turning several times during cooking. Avoid burning the chicken. Alternatively, you can cook the chicken in the oven at 180°C/350°F/Gas Mark 4 for 25 minutes.

Chicken & vegetables with a gherkin & mustard sauce

You can adapt this very French dish to your taste by changing the vegetables.

SERVES 2

1 large carrot, cut into sixths

2 sticks celery, peeled and quartered

4 medium mushrooms, halved

2 chicken pieces, skin and visible fat removed

salt and freshly ground black pepper

1 small leek, halved lengthwise
   and quartered

250 ml (9 fl oz) water

1 tablespoon chopped gherkins

1 tablespoon chopped parsley

1 spring onion, finely sliced

1 teaspoon Dijon mustard

In a large saucepan place the carrot, celery and mushrooms. Put the chicken on top, season with a little salt and pepper and top with the leeks. Pour over the water and bring to a simmer. Cover tightly with a lid and cook for about 25 minutes until the chicken is cooked.

Transfer the cooking liquid to a small saucepan. Bring to the boil and reduce the liquid by half. Stir in the gherkins, parsley, spring onion and mustard.

To serve, place the chicken and vegetables onto plates and spoon over the sauce.

Pan-fried chicken fillet with Madeira sauce & vegetables

This dish illustrates how to make a delicious and light low-fat sauce.
Trim off all chicken fat and skin and use a non-stick frying pan.

SERVES 2

1 medium carrot, peeled and
  cut into small sticks

1 stick celery, peeled and cut
  into small sticks

125 ml (4 fl oz) water

1 teaspoon olive oil

2 skinned chicken fillets

100 g (3½ oz) mushrooms, sliced

1 tablespoon dry Madeira

1 teaspoon cornflour mixed
  with 1 tablespoon water

salt and freshly ground black pepper

1 tablespoon chopped parsley

Place the carrots and celery into a saucepan with the water. Bring to the boil, cover with a tight-fitting lid and cook on low heat for about 5 minutes or until the vegetables are tender.

Heat the oil in a non-stick pan and brown the chicken on one side for about 4 minutes. Turn the chicken, cover with foil or a lid and cook for a further 5 minutes. Transfer the chicken to plates and keep warm. Add mushrooms to the pan and cook on high heat for 2 minutes. Add the Madeira, bring to the boil and add the cooking juices from the vegetables. Return to the boil and stir in the cornflour and water mixture to thicken the sauce slightly. Season with salt, pepper and parsley.

To serve, place the vegetables around the chicken and spoon over the sauce.

Chicken curry with vegetables

Cooking a curry is very pleasurable, especially when the spices release their exotic aroma into the kitchen. It is easier to make a curry in a wok in which the food can be easily mixed.

SERVES 4

½ onion

2 cm (¾ in) piece of ginger

2 cloves garlic

1 tablespoon groundnut oil

½ teaspoon fennel seeds

¼ teaspoon cumin seeds

2 teaspoons curry powder

3 tomatoes, chopped

4–6 skinless chicken pieces on the bone such as thighs or drumsticks

150 g (5 oz) mushrooms, sliced

200 g (7 oz) cauliflower, divided into small florets

200 g (7 oz) baby spinach leaves

½ teaspoon hot chilli paste

Blend the onion, ginger and garlic to a fine purée. Alternatively, chop finely by hand.

Heat up a wok and add the oil. When the oil is hot, add the fennel seeds, cumin seeds and puréed onion, ginger and garlic. Cook on medium heat without browning for 3–4 minutes. Add the curry powder and stir well for about 30 seconds. Then add the tomatoes. Bring to a simmer, add the chicken pieces and stir well. Cover and simmer for 10 minutes.

Stir the curry well and add the mushrooms and cauliflower. Stir again. Cover and cook for a further 15 minutes.

Add the spinach, cover and cook until it has softened – this takes only a few minutes. Stir in the chilli paste and serve.

Stir-fried chicken with mangetout & cloud ear mushrooms

Cloud ear mushroom or *wun yee* is a mushroom that is very popular with Chinese families. It is now sold fresh in Asian foodstores, but the dried ones work just as well.

SERVES 4

about 3 tablespoons dried cloud ear mushrooms (*wun yee*)

400 g (14 oz) skinless chicken fillets or thigh meat, cut into ½ cm (about ¼ in) slices across the grain

1 teaspoon sugar

a pinch of salt

2 teaspoons cornflour

1 tablespoon shaoshing wine (Chinese rice wine) *or* dry sherry

3 tablespoons light soy sauce

2 tablespoons groundnut oil

400 g (14 oz) mangetout, topped and tailed

3 thin slices fresh ginger

2 spring onions, cut into 1 cm (⅓ in) pieces

an extra 1 teaspoon cornflour mixed with 2 tablespoons water

1 teaspoon sesame oil

Soak the mushrooms in a bowl of boiling water from the kettle. When almost cold, drain and rinse under cold water. Trim away any hard bits.

Toss the chicken strips in a bowl with the sugar, salt, cornflour, wine and half a tablespoon of the soy sauce.

Add 2 teaspoons of the groundnut oil to a hot wok and, when oil is hot, stir-fry the mangetout and mushrooms on high heat for about 1 minute. If it starts to burn, add 1 tablespoon cold water. Transfer to a bowl.

Heat the remaining oil in the wok and stir in the ginger and spring onion. Add the marinated chicken and stir-fry on high heat for about 2 minutes. Stir in the cornflour mixed with water, remaining soy sauce and the sesame oil. Return the vegetables to the wok and toss well to combine the flavours. Serve immediately.

Mediterranean-style chicken casserole

Use skinless chicken pieces on the bone for this delicious dish.
You can prepare the dish one day in advance if you wish.

SERVES 3

1 tablespoon olive oil

3–6 skinless chicken pieces on the
    bone such as drumsticks or thighs

½ onion, chopped

2 sprigs of lemon thyme

1 green pepper, seeded and cut
    into eighths

3 tomatoes, finely chopped

½ glass dry white wine

100 g (3½ oz) mushrooms, halved

6 pitted black olives (optional)

salt and freshly ground black pepper

1 clove garlic, finely chopped

1 tablespoon finely sliced basil

Heat the oil in a non-stick saucepan and, on medium heat, brown the chicken pieces for 1 minute on each side. Transfer to a plate.

Add onion and thyme to the pan and, on medium heat, stir-fry for 2 minutes. Add the capsicum and stir-fry for 2 minutes. Add the tomatoes and stir well before adding the wine, mushrooms, olives and chicken pieces.

Season with a little salt and pepper and bring to a simmer. Cover and cook for about 20 minutes.

Just before serving, stir in the garlic and basil.

Chicken couscous

Couscous is one of my all-time favourite dishes to share
with good friends. Here is a Tunisian version.

SERVES 6–8

6–12 chicken drumsticks, skinned

a handful of Swiss chard leaves, shredded

3–4 sprigs of parsley

4 tablespoons tomato pureé

1 tablespoon ground cumin

1 tablespoon harissa *or*
Asian-style chilli paste

4 tablespoons olive oil

6 medium carrots, peeled
and quartered

4 turnips, peeled and quartered

2 red or green peppers, halved,
seeded and quartered

2 litres (3½ pints) water *or* chicken
stock (p. 204)

salt and freshly ground black pepper

200 g (7oz) can cooked chickpeas, drained

675 g (1lb 8oz) couscous

Place the drumsticks, Swiss chard leaves, parsley, tomato pureé, cumin, harissa, olive oil, carrots, turnips and pepper in a saucepan. Stir briefly to mix then add the stock and season with salt and pepper. Bring to the boil, cover and simmer for 30 minutes.

Add the cooked chickpeas and cook for a further 15 minutes.

Place the couscous in a fine strainer and run cold water over it for a few minutes. Place a damp cloth or piece of muslin in the perforated compartment of your steamer. Place the wet couscous on the cloth and bring the water in the steamer to the boil. Steam the couscous, uncovered, for about 10 minutes until the grains are soft.

Spoon the couscous onto a large platter and spoon about one-quarter of the juices over it with some of the vegetables. Serve the remaining vegetables, meat and juices in a separate bowl.

I recommend that
beginners try this
simple casserole.
It's guaranteed to
impress your dinner
party guests

Chicken in Red-wine sauce with carrots

I have modified this superb French classic to make it lighter and more digestible. It is a very enjoyable dish to cook and can be prepared in advance.

SERVES 4

8 small chicken thighs, skinned or other chicken pieces on the bone

a little plain flour

about 1 tablespoon groundnut oil

1 small onion, peeled and finely diced

1 stick celery, finely diced

1 rasher lean bacon, cut into small strips

12 small mushrooms

1 tablespoon brandy

1 glass red wine

250 ml (9 fl oz) chicken stock

1 clove garlic, crushed

125 ml (4 fl oz) Italian-style tomato sauce,   bottled or home-made (p. 210)

1 small bay leaf

freshly ground black pepper

2 medium carrots, peeled and cut into bite-size pieces

115 g (4 oz) shelled peas

1 tablespoon chopped parsley

Coat the chicken thighs with a little flour.

Heat two medium saucepans with 2 teaspoons of oil in each. In one pan, fry the onion and celery for 3–4 minutes on medium heat. In the second pan, fry the bacon for 2 minutes. Transfer the bacon to a bowl. In the empty pan, brown the chicken thighs. Transfer the browned chicken to the pan containing the celery and onion. In the empty saucepan cook the mushrooms on high heat for about 5 minutes. Transfer the mushrooms to a bowl.

Add brandy to the pan and bring to the boil. Add the wine, stock and garlic, and return to the boil. Add the tomato sauce and when it comes to a simmer, pour this liquid over the chicken and stir well, adding the bay leaf and seasoning with a little pepper. Add carrots to the chicken, stir, cover and cook for about 25 minutes.

Stir in the peas and cook uncovered for a further 10 minutes. Then add the bacon, mushrooms and chopped parsley. Stir through and serve.

Rabbit casserole with prunes

Rabbit is one of the most flavoursome meats and you can now buy rabbit pieces from good poultry shops. This dish is simple to prepare but takes 1½ hours to cook.

SERVES 2

2 teaspoons groundnut oil

2 rabbit hind legs

1 sprig of thyme, finely chopped

¼ onion, diced

1 teaspoon tomato pureé

1 clove garlic, crushed

1 glass red wine

250 ml (9 fl oz) boiling water

10 prunes, pitted

salt and freshly ground black pepper

2 carrots, sliced

1 tablespoon chopped parsley

Heat the oil in a non-stick saucepan and brown the rabbit pieces. Add the thyme and onion, and stir for 1 minute before adding the tomato pureé, garlic and wine. Bring to the boil, add the boiling water and prunes, and season with salt and pepper. Lower to a simmer, cover and cook for 1 hour.

After 1 hour, add the carrots, cover and cook for a further 30 minutes. Check that the rabbit is tender. Cook a little longer if necessary.

Stir in the parsley and serve.

Chicken Satay

If barbecuing these satays on bamboo sticks, soak the sticks for at least 20 minutes in cold water before use to prevent them from burning. You will need about 6 bamboo sticks. Serve with a choice of salads. Sambal oelek is readily available from Asian foodstores.

SERVES 2

juice of ¼ lemon

1 teaspoon soy sauce

1 teaspoon honey

½ clove garlic, finely chopped

¼ teaspoon turmeric (optional)

¼ teaspoon paprika

¼ teaspoon ground cumin

¼ teaspoon chilli paste (sambal oelek), or to taste

1 teaspoon groundnut oil

a little freshly ground black pepper

250 g (9 oz) deboned, skinned chicken meat, cut into bite-sized pieces

2 lemon wedges or peanut sauce (p. 207)

To make the marinade, in a medium bowl combine the lemon juice, soy sauce, honey, garlic, turmeric, paprika, cumin, chilli paste, oil and pepper. Toss chicken in this marinade and refrigerate until required. Marinate the chicken for several hours but for no more than 6 hours.

Thread the meat onto skewers and cook under the grill. Alternatively, cook either in a frying pan brushed with a little oil, on a barbecue or on a rack in a hot oven. The satays will take only a few minutes to cook. Be careful not to overcook; the satays are much tastier moist than hard and dry.

Serve with lemon wedges or with peanut sauce.

Roast Christmas Turkey

It is great fun cooking a large roast for a special occasion. All you need to remember
is to cook the turkey a little ahead of time and allow it to rest before carving.
The bread and orange stuffing, which can be made the day before, is delicious,
and keeps the meat moist during cooking. It can be omitted if you like.

SERVES 8–12

1 quantity of bread and
orange stuffing (p. 155)

3.5 kg (about 7½ lb) turkey

3 tablespoons olive oil

4 sprigs of thyme, finely
chopped

salt and freshly ground
black pepper

1 large onion, cut into sixths

1 large carrot, diced

3 tablespoons brandy

1 glass dry white wine

500 ml (18 fl oz) water or chicken
stock (p. 204)

2 teaspoons cornflour mixed
with 2 tablespoons water

3 tablespoons chopped parsley
or tarragon or basil

Preheat the oven to 150°C/300°F/Gas Mark 2.

Place three-quarters of the stuffing inside the cleaned and emptied
cavity of the turkey. Place the remaining stuffing in the wishbone cavity
under the skin and neck. Truss the thighs with kitchen string to hold the
stuffing inside.

Mix the olive oil with the thyme and a little salt and pepper and brush
the turkey with it. Place the turkey on one side in your largest roasting
tray on an oven rack. Roast the turkey in the preheated oven for about
45 minutes and turn to other side. Add the onion and carrot to the
roasting tray and roast for a further 45 minutes. Turn the turkey onto its
back, baste with the cooking juices and cook for a further 30–40
minutes. Pierce the thickest part of the turkey with a skewer to check if
it's done – the juices should run clear.

Remove the turkey from the oven, place on a large serving dish, cover
with foil and leave to rest for at least 15 minutes or until ready to serve.

Drain the fat from the roasting tray and place the tray on medium heat
on top of the stove. Add the brandy and stir with the vegetables in the
tray to extract as much flavour as possible. Add the wine and bring to
the boil. Add the stock, raise the heat, and simmer for 5 minutes. Strain
the sauce into a small saucepan. Discard the vegetables. Bring the
sauce to the boil and whisk in the cornflour and water mixture. The
sauce will thicken a little. Season with salt and pepper and stir in the
parsley before serving.

Serve each person with a thin slice of turkey breast, a little stuffing and
a small piece of leg meat. Spoon over a little gravy. Merry Christmas!

Bread & orange stuffing

I have enjoyed this stuffing ever since I was a little boy, when my grandmother used to make it to stuff turkey, chicken, river fish and tomatoes. This quantity is sufficient to stuff a 3.5 kg (about 7½ lb) turkey.

SERVES 10

600 g (1¼ lb) wholemeal bread,
  cut into small pieces

750 ml (1¼ pints) milk

1 tablespoon olive oil

1 large onion, finely chopped

2 cloves garlic, crushed

1 tablespoon finely grated orange rind

1 tablespoon butter *or* 1 tablespoon
  extra-virgin olive oil

3 tablespoons brandy

juice of ½ lemon

4 tablespoons chopped parsley
  or tarragon *or* basil

salt and freshly ground black pepper

Place the bread in a bowl. Bring the milk to the boil and pour over the bread. Allow to soak.

Heat the oil in a non-stick saucepan and over medium heat stir-fry the onion for about 5 minutes or until soft. Add the garlic, stir for 1 minute, then stir in the orange rind. Add the bread and milk preparation, lower the heat and mix until a sticky paste forms. Mix in the butter, brandy, lemon juice and parsley. Season with salt and pepper and remove from the heat.

You can use the stuffing immediately or allow to cool and refrigerate. Use within 1 day.

Most of us love the flavour of beef, lamb and pork, and in recent times butchers have dramatically changed the way they cut and present meat. The cuts on offer now are smaller and leaner than they were 10 years ago. A moderate serving of lean meat of about 90 g (3¼ oz) per person, cooked in a minimum of fat and served with plenty of vegetables makes a good occasional meal. In the context of this book, which aims to reduce the risk of cancers related to what we eat, try to avoid eating beef and lamb fat, burning the meat during cooking, browning it too much or overcooking. Take care especially when you cook on the barbecue. Make sure your barbecue is very clean and preheat it well before starting. Don't cook over an open flame and avoid squeezing the juices out of the meat and moving the meat around as it cooks. Serve the meat as soon as it is cooked.

meat

Pan-fried or grilled steak

This is the basic method of cooking a steak. Buy a piece of steak about 2.5 cm (1 in) thick and weighing no more than 150 g (5 oz) per person. Buy the steak on the day you cook it and avoid keeping for more than 2 days. If you are unsure about the freshness, just smell it. Any off smell indicates it's no longer fresh.

SERVES 1

about 1 teaspoon groundnut or olive oil

150 g (5 oz) steak, trimmed

a little salt (optional)

freshly ground black pepper

Brush a grill or non-stick pan with oil and place on medium heat for about 1 minute. Place the steak on the grill or pan. Avoid moving or poking the steak during cooking.

If you like your steak medium-rare, turn after 3 minutes and cook the other side for a further 2–3 minutes. If you prefer your steak well-done, cook it for 5 minutes on one side before turning it over and cooking for a further 4–5 minutes. Avoid burning the steak, and increase or decrease the heat as you feel necessary. When the steak is cooked, transfer to a plate, season with salt and pepper and serve.

Steak with tomato & olive sauce

If you have no Italian-style tomato sauce, use half a can of peeled, chopped tomatoes. Some of the sauce ingredients are quite salty so no added salt is necessary. Serve with steamed vegetables.

SERVES 2

2 teaspoons olive oil

2 x 150 g (5 oz) lean steaks such as rump, porterhouse or fillet

1 clove garlic, chopped

1 anchovy fillet, chopped (optional)

4 capers, chopped

125 ml (4 fl oz) Italian-style tomato sauce, bottled or home-made (p. 210)

6 black olives, pitted

1 tablespoon chopped parsley or finely sliced basil

freshly ground black pepper

Heat the olive oil in a non-stick frying pan and on medium heat cook the steaks for 3–5 minutes on each side. Refer to the instructions for pan-fried steak for approximate cooking times. When the steaks are cooked to your liking, transfer to a serving dish and cover with foil.

With the pan on low heat add the garlic, anchovy and capers and fry for 30 seconds. Stir in the tomato sauce and olives, increase the heat, and bring to the boil. Add the parsley and season with pepper. Serve the sauce on or around the steaks.

Stir-fried beef with ginger & chinese cabbage

You can use any vegetable in this popular dish but I find that
Chinese cabbage works really well, since it absorbs the flavourings nicely.

SERVES 2

2 teaspoons shaoshing wine (Chinese
   rice wine) or dry sherry

1 teaspoon cornflour

freshly ground black pepper

2 teaspoons cold water

200 g (7 oz) very lean beef such as skirt
   or rump

1 tablespoon groundnut oil

about 200 g (7 oz) Chinese cabbage,
   finely shredded

1 clove garlic, finely sliced

2 teaspoons grated ginger

2 teaspoons low-salt soy sauce

1/2 teaspoon sesame oil

To make the marinade, combine the rice wine with the
cornflour, pepper and cold water in a medium bowl.

Cut the beef into 1/2 cm (1/4 in) slices across the grain.
Place in the marinade and allow to sit for at least
10 minutes.

Pour a third of the groundnut oil into a hot wok and stir-
fry the cabbage for about 5 minutes or until soft. If it
starts burning, pour 1 tablespoon of water down the
side of the wok. Transfer the cabbage to a bowl.

Heat the remaining oil in the wok and stir in the garlic
and ginger. Add the beef and stir-fry on high heat for
about 20–30 seconds until it changes colour. Stir in the
soy sauce, return the cabbage to the pan and toss to
mix through. Just before serving, stir in the sesame oil.

Meatballs with sauce

This lovely dish can be served with pasta, noodles, rice, steamed potatoes or polenta.
Buy the minced beef on the day you make the dish or no earlier than one day before.
If you wish, you can use chicken, veal or pork mince instead.

SERVES 4

400 g (14 oz) lean ground beef

4 tablespoons breadcrumbs

3 tablespoons cold water

2 cloves garlic, chopped

3 tablespoons chopped parsley

1 tablespoon finely sliced basil

1 egg

salt and freshly ground black pepper

a little plain flour

1 tablespoon olive oil

3 tablespoons dry white *or* red wine
or 2 teaspoons brandy

about 500 ml (18 fl oz) Italian-style
tomato sauce, bottled or home-made
(p. 210)

1 teaspoon finely grated or
chopped orange rind

In a bowl, and using your hands, thoroughly combine the ground beef with the breadcrumbs, water, half the garlic, half the parsley, half the basil and egg. Season and combine a little more.

Form the mince into small balls about the size of golf balls, dipping your hands in water after each one. Coat each ball lightly with flour.

Heat the oil in a wide, non-stick frying pan and on medium heat brown the meatballs for about 1 minute on each side. Add the wine to the pan and bring to the boil. Add the tomato sauce and orange rind, bring to a simmer and cook for about 8 minutes, stirring the meatballs occasionally and spooning over the sauce to keep them moist. Stir in the remaining garlic, parsley and basil, season with black pepper and serve.

Mexican-style meatloaf

This meatloaf has the Mexican flavours of cumin and chilli. It can be enjoyed
with an Italian-style tomato sauce and I like to serve it with mashed potatoes and a green salad.
You need a greased loaf tin.

SERVES 8

1 tablespoon olive oil

¼ teaspoon cumin seeds

115 g (4 oz) finely diced carrots

55 g (2 oz) finely diced red pepper

115 g (4 oz) finely diced aubergine

55 g (2 oz) shelled peas

½ teaspoon ground cumin

125 ml (4 fl oz) water

800 g (1¾ lb) ground lean beef

55 g (2 oz) fresh breadcrumbs

½ teaspoon hot chilli paste

a little salt and freshly ground
   black pepper

1 tablespoon tomato ketchup

Heat the oil in a large non-stick frying pan and gently
stir-fry the cumin seeds, carrots and pepper for
1 minute. Add the aubergine, peas and ground cumin,
stir and cook for 2 minutes. Add half the water and cook
for a further 2 minutes. Allow to cool a little.

Preheat the oven to 220°C/425°F/Gas Mark 7.

Mix the ground beef with the breadcrumbs, cooked
vegetables, remaining water, chilli paste and a little
salt and pepper. Mix thoroughly for about 1 minute,
spoon the preparation into a greased loaf tin and
brush the top with ketchup. Bake in a preheated
oven for 20 minutes, then lower the temperature to
180°C/350°F/Gas Mark 4 and cook for a further
20 minutes.

Remove the meatloaf from the oven and leave to rest
for 10 minutes before carefully slicing with a serrated
knife.

Steak & kidney casserole with carrots

This dish, a modern version of a popular classic, practically cooks itself and is delicious served with plenty of carrots. To keep the dish healthy, it is important to trim the meat of all fat. It takes about 2 hours to cook.

SERVES 2

about 150 g (5 oz) lean casserole beef, trimmed and cubed

about 150 g (5 oz) lean beef kidney, trimmed and cubed

2 teaspoons plain flour

salt and freshly ground black pepper

2 teaspoons groundnut oil

½ onion, finely diced

2 sprigs of parsley, roughly chopped

125 ml (4 fl oz) Italian-style tomato sauce, bottled or home-made (p. 210)

4 tablespoons red wine

125 ml (4 fl oz) water

1 clove garlic, crushed

2 large carrots, cut into bite-size pieces

Mix the beef and kidney with the flour, a little salt and black pepper.

Preheat the oven to 180°C/350°F/Gas Mark 4.

Heat the oil in an ovenproof casserole dish and gently fry the onion for about 5 minutes. Switch off the heat and add the beef, kidney and parsley. Add the tomato sauce, wine, water and garlic without stirring. Place the carrots on top. Do not stir them in. Cover the pan with a layer of foil then with a lid. Cook in the preheated oven for about 2 hours.

Stir the beef, kidney and vegetables together just before serving. This dish is lovely with mashed potato.

This is a dish for
the more confident
cook.

Roast beef fillet with sweet vegetables

Although beef fillet is one of the dearest cuts of meat, there is little wastage. Here, the beef is stuffed with cooked vegetables.

SERVES 3

2 teaspoons olive oil

¼ teaspoon cumin seeds

½ onion, diced

about 300 g (11 oz) pumpkin flesh, cut into 1 cm (⅓ in) dice

about 300 g (11 oz) sweet potatoes, cut into 1 cm (⅓ in) dice

125 ml (4 fl oz) Italian-style tomato sauce, bottled or home-made (p. 210)

125 ml (4 fl oz) water

salt and freshly ground black pepper

a pinch of cayenne pepper

3 tablespoons chopped parsley

about 250 g (9 oz) peas, cooked and drained

450 g (almost 1 lb) piece of beef fillet

1 small carrot, diced

125 ml (4 fl oz) water

125 ml (4 fl oz) dry white wine

1 teaspoon cornflour mixed with 1 tablespoon water

Heat half the oil in a medium-sized pan. Stir in the cumin seeds and half of the onions and fry for 2 minutes. Add the pumpkin, sweet potatoes, tomato sauce and water. Cover and cook until the vegetables are tender. Drain the vegetables, reserving the juices. Season with a little salt, cayenne, black pepper and chopped parsley. Stir in the cooked peas. Cool.

Preheat the oven to 200°C/400°F/Gas Mark 6.

Using a small, sharp knife and starting at the smaller end of the fillet, make a little cut into the meat but don't slit right through to the other end. Fill this pocket with some of the vegetables.

Brush a small, heavy roasting tray with the remaining oil and, over high heat, brown the beef on all sides. Add the onion mixture and bake in the preheated oven for 15–20 minutes. Transfer to a warm serving platter, cover with foil and rest for about 10 minutes.

Place the roasting tray on medium heat and stir-fry the rest of the onion and carrot for 1 minute. Add the white wine, reserved vegetable juices and ½ cup water. Boil for 2–3 minutes then strain this into a small saucepan. Return to the boil and stir in the cornflour preparation. Season to taste.

Cut the beef into 3 slices. Spoon a little sauce onto each plate and top each with a slice of beef. Season with extra pepper and serve with the leftover vegetables.

Veal or Beef osso buco

This classic Italian dish, superb in winter, can be made with either veal or beef. Using veal will produce a more delicate dish than beef; it is, however, more expensive. Beef will also take about an hour longer to cook. Whichever you use, be sure to trim all visible fat from the meat. I suggest cooking the dish in a large saucepan or in an ovenproof dish.

SERVES 4

3 tablespoons olive oil

½ onion, finely chopped

1 medium carrot, finely chopped

1 stick celery, finely chopped

4–8 slices shin of veal *or* beef,
  cut into 3 cm (1½ in) slices

a little plain flour

125 ml (4 fl oz) dry white wine

250 ml (9 fl oz) beef *or* veal stock (p. 205)

400 g (14 oz) can peeled
  tomatoes, chopped

1 teaspoon tomato pureé

2 sprigs of thyme

1 clove garlic, crushed

salt and freshly ground black pepper

rind of ½ lemon, finely grated

3 tablespoons chopped parsley

Heat half the oil in a wide saucepan and cook the onion, carrot and celery for about 5 minutes. Transfer to a plate.

Lightly coat the veal or beef slices with flour. Heat the remaining oil in the pan and brown the meat on both sides for about 2 minutes on each side. Add the wine, stock, tomatoes, tomato paste, thyme and garlic to the pan. Season with a little salt and pepper and gently stir in the cooked onion, carrot and celery. Bring to a simmer, cover the pan and cook for about 1½ hours if you're using veal, and 2–2½ hours for beef. It can also be cooked in a preheated oven at 150°C/300°F/Gas Mark 2 for about the same duration.

Just before serving, stir in the lemon rind and chopped parsley.

Veal fillet with carrots & Fines Herbs

Veal fillet is lean, delicate and tender. Good butchers usually have quality veal, and it is always wise to order it in advance. Don't worry if you can't get all the herbs, but you must try it at least once with tarragon.

SERVES 4

600 g (1¼ lb) baby carrots, peeled and cut into bite-size pieces

125 ml (4 fl oz) water

1 teaspoon groundnut oil

about 600 g (1¼ lb) veal fillet, cut into 3 cm (1½ in) slices

salt and freshly ground black pepper

3 tablespoons port

250 ml (9 fl oz) veal (p. 205) or vegetable stock (p. 203)

1 teaspoon cornflour mixed with 3 tablespoons water

1 tablespoon finely chopped tarragon

1 tablespoon finely chopped parsley

about 18 small sprigs of chervil

Place the carrots in a saucepan with half a cup of water. Cover and cook until soft.

Heat the oil in a non-stick pan and cook the veal slices on both sides until just done. Each side takes about 3–4 minutes. Transfer the veal to a warm plate, season with a little salt and pepper, and keep warm under foil or a lid.

Add port to the pan and allow to reduce a little before adding the stock and all of the carrot cooking juices. Return to the boil and reduce the liquid to about 1 cup. Stir in the cornflour mixture and bring to a simmer. Toss the carrots in the sauce with the herbs and season.

Place the veal on plates with the carrots and spoon over the sauce. Garnish with sprigs of chervil and serve.

Lamb cutlets with thyme & tomatoes

Select very lean lamb cutlets and, if there are
none on display, ask your butcher to cut some up for you.
This dish is lovely with mashed potatoes.

SERVES 1

2 tomatoes, diced

2 teaspoons olive oil

½ clove garlic, finely chopped

1 sprig of thyme, finely chopped

3 lean lamb cutlets, trimmed

salt and freshly ground black pepper

juice of ¼ lemon

Mix the tomato with half of the oil, the garlic and half of the thyme.

Sprinkle cutlets with the remaining thyme. Heat the remaining oil in a non-stick frying pan and cook the cutlets for 3 minutes on one side. Turn, and cook for about 2 minutes on the other. Transfer to a plate and season with salt and pepper.

Add the tomato mixture to the pan, increase the heat and stir for 1 minute. Spoon over the meat and serve sprinkled with lemon juice.

Lamb steak with courgettes & Roast pumpkin

With the new cuts of lamb available,
butchers now sell lean lamb steaks taken from the leg.
Serve with a green salad or a green vegetable.

SERVES 2

about 1 tablespoon olive oil

½ clove garlic, finely chopped

1 teaspoon chopped rosemary
  or thyme

2 x 150 g (5 oz) lamb steaks,
  trimmed of fat

about 250 g (9 oz) butternut pumpkin
  or other pumpkin of your choice,
  skin on, cut into 1 cm (⅓ in) slices

¼ teaspoon sweet paprika

salt and freshly ground black pepper

2 courgettes, cut diagonally into
  ½ cm (¼ in) slices

juice of ¼ lemon

Preheat the oven to 220°C/425°F/Gas Mark 7.

Combine half the oil, the garlic and the rosemary in a bowl and brush the lamb steaks with this marinade. Leave to marinate while you prepare the vegetables.

Place the pumpkin on an oven tray lined with baking paper (optional) and brush the pumpkin lightly with a little oil seasoned with paprika and pepper. Bake in the preheated oven for about 20 minutes, turning over halfway through.

Five minutes before the pumpkin is ready, brush a non-stick pan or grill with the remaining olive oil and cook the lamb for about 3 minutes on medium heat. Turn the meat and cook the other side for a further 3 minutes. Remove from the pan and place in the oven with the pumpkin.

Add the courgettes to the pan or grill and cook on each side for about 1 minute. Serve the pumpkin on plates topped with meat. Season to taste, and top with the courgettes. Drizzle over the lemon juice and serve.

Grilled loin of lamb provençale

This dish was inspired by a visit to the south of France. For the presentation of the dish I used a piece of PVC pipe of about 10 cm (4 in) in diameter and 5 cm (2 in) high to arrange the vegetables and meat neatly. Alternatively, you can use a round pastry cutter about 10 cm (4 in) in diameter. I usually cook the meat on a cast-iron grill but it can be cooked in a pan.

SERVES 2

2 deboned racks of lamb, each containing 4 chops, trimmed

2 sprigs of lemon thyme, finely chopped

1 tablespoon olive oil

salt and freshly ground black pepper

1 tomato, diced

a few basil leaves, finely sliced

1 clove garlic, finely chopped

½ red pepper, sliced

150 g (5 oz) mushrooms, sliced

about 100 g (3½ oz) baby spinach leaves

a pinch of cayenne pepper

Season the meat with half the lemon thyme, 1 teaspoon oil and a little pepper.

Mix the tomato in a bowl with 1 teaspoon of oil, the remaining lemon thyme, basil and garlic.

Heat the remaining oil in a non-stick pan and on low heat stir-fry the pepper for 1 minute. Add the mushrooms, increase the heat and stir-fry for 1 minute. Add the spinach and stir until wilted. Season with salt, pepper and cayenne pepper.

Preheat the grill to medium and, when hot, cook the lamb for about 4 minutes on each side. Season with pepper, and leave to rest for 3 or 4 minutes before serving. Slice the meat if you wish.

To serve, place the PVC rings (or pastry cutters) on plates and spoon the vegetables into the rings. Top with the meat and lift off. Spoon the tomato sauce around and serve.

Loin of lamb with Green flageolet beans

Green flageolet beans are one of the most delicious beans. If fresh ones
are not available, you can get the canned variety in gourmet shops and delis.
The French love to serve lamb and flageolet beans together, along with a green salad.

SERVES 6

900 g (almost 2 lb) loin of lamb,
  trimmed

3 tablespoons olive oil

1 tablespoon chopped rosemary

salt and freshly ground black pepper

about 300 g (11 oz) pumpkin,
  cut into 1 cm (1/3 in) slices

1 small carrot, diced

1 small onion, diced

about 300 g (11 oz) French beans

400 g (14 oz) can green
  flageolet beans

1 teaspoon tomato pureé

4 tablespoons red wine

1 clove garlic, crushed

250 ml (9 fl oz) beef stock (p. 205)

Preheat the oven to 200°C/400°F/Gas Mark 6.

Coat the lamb with half of the oil and the rosemary and
season with pepper.

Heat the remaining oil in a roasting tray and brown the
meat and pumpkin pieces for a few minutes on high
heat. Add the carrot and onion, place in the preheated
oven and roast for 15 minutes.

Steam or microwave the French beans and reheat the
flageolet beans in their juices.

Transfer the meat and pumpkin to a plate, season with
salt and cover.

Place the roasting tray on medium heat, and stir the
tomato pureé into the remaining vegetables in the
roasting tray. Stir in the wine and garlic. Bring to the
boil. Add the stock and boil for 2 minutes before
straining the sauce into a small saucepan.

To serve, pour a little sauce onto hot plates and top
with the sliced meat, vegetables and beans.

Roast leg of lamb with gravy

Many men I spoke to have nominated this as their favourite meal. It is best to trim the meat of as much fat as possible and to avoid overcooking the meat so as to keep it tender. Serve with roast vegetables and a steamed green vegetable or a salad. Roast the vegetables in a separate oven tray.

SERVES 8

1.5 kg (3 lb) leg of lamb, trimmed

2 cloves garlic, peeled and quartered

3 tablespoons olive oil

1/4 teaspoon chilli paste (optional)

1 tablespoon finely chopped thyme

salt and freshly ground black pepper

1 carrot, coarsely diced

1 onion, coarsely diced

1 teaspoon tomato pureé

125 ml (4 fl oz) dry white wine

250 ml (9 fl oz) water

2 teaspoons cornflour mixed with
   1 tablespoon white wine

1 tablespoon chopped parsley

Preheat the oven to 180°C/350°F/Gas Mark 4.

Using the tip of a small blade, make eight small cuts into the lamb at regular intervals, ensuring that the cuts are deep enough for the garlic slivers. The garlic must not protrude from the meat.

Mix the olive oil with the chilli paste and thyme, and brush the lamb all over with the mixture. Season with black pepper, and place on a rack and sit in a roasting tray. Roast the lamb for about 50 minutes, turning it two or three times during cooking so that it cooks evenly.

Twenty minutes after the start of the cooking, add the diced carrot and onion to the tray.

When the meat is done, remove from the oven. Place on a dish, cover with foil and leave to rest for about 10 minutes before serving.

To make your gravy, drain as much fat as possible from the tray. Keep the onions and carrots in the tray. Place on medium heat and stir in the tomato pureé. Add the wine and boil to reduce the juices by half. Add the water, bring to the boil and whisk in the cornflour mixture. Add any meat juices from the plate and season the gravy with salt and pepper. Strain into a small saucepan and keep warm. Discard the carrots, onions and herbs. Slice the meat and serve with the gravy and parsley.

Couscous with Grilled Lamb kebabs

Couscous is a coarse wheat semolina, very popular in North African countries
and in the south of Italy. The cooking instructions on the pack usually suggest
cooking couscous in hot water but I find that steaming gives a lighter result.
You will need to soak 2 bamboo skewers in cold water for about 30 minutes before using.

SERVES 2

250 g (9 oz) lean lamb meat
  from the leg, cubed

1 tablespoon olive oil

1 teaspoon ground cumin

1 clove garlic, finely chopped

1 teaspoon harissa *or* Asian-style
  chilli paste (sambal oelek)

salt and freshly ground black pepper

1 long carrot, peeled and quartered

1 turnip, peeled and quartered

½ red pepper, seeded and quartered

1 courgette, halved

2 tomatoes, quartered

2 teaspoons tomato pureé

500 ml (18 fl oz) water

55 g (2 oz) cooked chickpeas, drained

150 g (5 oz) couscous

a few sprigs of fresh coriander (garnish)

Place the lamb cubes in a bowl and mix with half the oil, half the cumin, half the garlic, half the harissa and a little pepper.

To a large saucepan add the carrot, turnip, pepper, courgette, tomatoes, tomato pureé, water and the remaining oil, cumin, garlic and harissa. Season and bring to the boil. Lower to a simmer and cook for 15 minutes.

Add the drained chickpeas and cook for a further 10 minutes.

To prepare the couscous, place the couscous in a fine strainer and run cold water over it for a few minutes. Place a damp cloth or piece of muslin over the perforated compartment of your steamer. Place the damp couscous in the steamer on top of the cloth and bring the water in the steamer to the boil. Steam the couscous, uncovered, for about 10 minutes until the grains are soft.

Preheat the grill. Thread the lamb cubes onto skewers. Place the meat on the grill for about 8 minutes, turning the kebabs twice during the cooking.

Place the couscous in a serving dish with the kebabs on top. Garnish with the coriander. Serve the vegetables and juices in a bowl from the centre of the table for all to help themselves.

Stir-fried vegetables with Roast pork

You may have seen displayed in the windows of many Chinese restaurants
or take-aways the appetizing red-coloured roasted strips of lean pork.
These are sold by weight, and you can ask for them to be sliced or left whole.
Ask for a whole piece, unsliced, for this recipe.

SERVES 2

2 teaspoons groundnut oil

¼ teaspoon sesame oil

1 teaspoon grated ginger

1 clove garlic, sliced

about 100 g (3½ oz) cabbage,
    finely sliced

100 g (3½ oz) sugar-snap peas *or*
    mangetout, topped and tailed

100 g (3½ oz) mushrooms of
    your choice, finely sliced

8 baby corn cobs from a can, drained

about 250 g (9 oz) Chinese roast
    pork, sliced diagonally into
    bite-size pieces

2 teaspoons low-salt soy sauce

¼ teaspoon chilli paste

2 spring onions, finely sliced

a few sprigs of fresh coriander

Heat the wok and add the groundnut and sesame oils.
Stir in the ginger and garlic and immediately add
the cabbage. Stir-fry for 30 seconds. Add about
1 tablespoon cold water down the side of the wok if
the cabbage starts sticking or burning. Add the sugar-
snap peas and stir-fry for 30 seconds. Then add the
mushrooms and baby corn, and stir-fry until the
vegetables are soft.

Stir in the pork, soy sauce and chilli paste, and stir to
distribute the flavours and heat through. If you wish,
you could reheat the pork in the oven and serve it on
top of the stir-fried vegetables. Serve sprinkled with
spring onion and coriander leaves.

Lamb shanks with vegetables

This great winter classic is full of flavour and texture. It is best cooked in an ovenproof casserole and takes about 2 hours. If you are short of time, cook it in a pressure cooker, in which case reduce the cooking time to around 40 minutes. As the dish is rich, select small shanks.

SERVES 4

1 tablespoon olive oil

4 lamb shanks, trimmed of all visible fat

3 sprigs of thyme

½ onion, chopped

1 tablespoon red wine vinegar or
    125 ml (4 fl oz) dry white wine

375 ml (13 fl oz) Italian-style tomato sauce,
    bottled or home-made (p. 210)

250 ml (9 fl oz) water

1 clove garlic, crushed

8 baby carrots, peeled and left whole

2 sticks celery, cut into 5 cm (2 in) pieces

1 red pepper, halved and cut into eighths

salt and freshly ground black pepper

Preheat the oven to 150°C/300°F/Gas Mark 2.

Heat the oil in a large casserole dish and brown the shanks for a few minutes. Add the thyme and onion, and stir for 2 minutes. Add the vinegar, tomato sauce and water, and shake the pan a little before adding the garlic, whole carrots, celery and pepper.

Season with a little salt and pepper and stir well. Bring to a simmer, cover and cook in the preheated oven for about 2 hours or until the meat comes away from the bone.

Serve with boiled potatoes.

Stir-fried pork with shredded vegetables

For this quick dish, I use pork fillet, but you can also use pork loin or
a cut that butchers sell as pork steak. When shredding the vegetables,
cut them into long thin strips, about the size of the bean sprouts.

SERVES 2

1 tablespoon groundnut oil

2 teaspoons grated ginger

about 100 g (3½ oz) Chinese
    cabbage (*wong nga bak*)

about 100 g (3½ oz) bean sprouts

1 stick tender celery, cut into
    6 cm (2 in) strips

2 mushrooms, finely sliced

1 medium carrot, cut into
    6 cm (2 in) strips

1 clove garlic, finely sliced

200 g (7 oz) pork fillet or
    very lean pork, sliced

2 teaspoons low-salt soy sauce

½ teaspoon sesame oil

¼ teaspoon chilli paste (optional)

a few sprigs of fresh coriander

Heat a wok and, when hot, add a third of the oil. Add
the ginger, cabbage, bean sprouts, celery, mushroom
and carrot and stir-fry until soft. If the mixture starts to
burn or stick to the pan, add 2 tablespoons water down
the side of the wok. Transfer the vegetables to a plate.

Heat the remaining oil in the wok. Add the garlic and
pork, and stir-fry until the pork changes colour. Stir in the
soy sauce, sesame oil and chilli. Return the vegetables
to the pan and reheat well. Serve garnished with
coriander leaves.

Desserts

JAM

Rich desserts containing lots of cream, butter and chocolate are a nice treat for special occasions. On a daily basis, however, desserts can be seen as a way to complement the rest of the day's diet. So treat yourself to delicious seasonal fruits by eating grapes in autumn, oranges in winter, strawberries in spring and summer, and so on. For more special treats, learn to make luscious fruit salads – there are a few lovely ones in this chapter. During winter, fruits can also be stewed and eaten over a few days. And remember that dried fruits such as figs and apricots, and nuts such as walnuts and almonds make delightful desserts.

Low-fat dairy products such as yoghurt and cottage cheese are a good source of calcium. Low-fat puddings and slices are a nice way to finish a meal, as are pancakes. If you must have cream or ice-cream, be moderate in your servings.

Sweet creamy topping

This is a delicious alternative to cream and ice-cream. Serve with fruit salads or fruit desserts. I use a fresh low-fat cream cheese with a fat content of less than 8 per cent. Manufacturers call this cheese quark or fromage frais.

SERVES 4

5 tablespoons fromage frais

4 tablespoons low-fat milk

2 teaspoons castor sugar *or* honey

1 teaspoon finely grated lemon *or* orange rind *or* a pinch of ground cinnamon *or* 2 drops pure vanilla essence

Whisk or blend all the ingredients to a creamy consistency and refrigerate until required.

Dates & orange on yoghurt

Oranges with dates and yoghurt are a refreshing and nourishing way to finish a meal.

SERVES 6–8

1 kg (2lb 4oz) low-fat natural yoghurt

3 tablespoons milk

3 tablespoons orange marmalade

3 tablespoons chopped almonds

1 orange, sliced or segmented

8–16 dates

Place the yoghurt, milk and marmalade in a bowl and whip together until smooth. Pour into a large dish. Sprinkle with almonds and top with orange slices and dates. Refrigerate until required.

Williams pears & passionfruit Salad

For this easy, light, luscious dessert select Williams pears that are just ripe,
that is, light green turning yellow. You can make the salad several hours in advance
but make sure the liquid covers or coats the pears.

SERVES 4–6

4 oranges or 375ml (13 fl oz) best-quality
orange juice

juice of ½ lemon

3 heavy passionfruit

3 tablespoons sugar *or* orange
blossom honey (optional)

4 just-ripe Williams pears

1 tablespoon kirsch *or* Drambuie *or*
brandy (optional)

Squeeze the oranges into a bowl. Mix in the lemon
juice, passionfruit pulp and sugar or honey.

Peel, quarter and core the pears. Cut each quarter into
3 segments and add to the juices. Cover the bowl with
plastic film and refrigerate.

Remove from the refrigerator 15 minutes before serving.
Stir in the liqueur of your choice and serve.

Fresh fruit platter with two berry sauces

You can serve a seasonal fruit platter at any time of the year. My favourite
time is the warmer months of the year when the berries are sweet and delicious.
In this recipe I serve the fruits with a blueberry and raspberry sauce.

SERVES 4

200 g (7 oz) punnet blueberries

200 g (7 oz) punnet raspberries

juice of 2 oranges

juice of 1 lemon

3 tablespoons sugar

a selection of seasonal fruits for the
platter: 4 apricots, 1 large peach,
1 large bunch of grapes, 1 mango,
½ pawpaw, 250 g (9 oz) berries

In a blender purée the blueberries and a quarter of
the raspberries with half the orange juice, half the
lemon juice and half the sugar. Strain the sauce into
a bowl and refrigerate until 5 minutes before serving.

Blend the remaining raspberries with the remaining
orange and lemon juices and sugar. Strain into a bowl
and refrigerate until 5 minutes before serving.

Prepare the fruits for the platter by washing, peeling
and slicing as necessary. Pile the fruits attractively on
a platter and accompany with the two berry sauces.

chef's note

Take time when
choosing pawpaw
Make sure it is
just ripe and
unblemished. If
not sure, ask your
greengrocer for he

Peach, mango & berry fruit salad in pawpaw

These fabulous fruits are available to us at the end of summer and
what a treat they are! You can easily adapt the recipe according to the
availability of the fruits and use, say, pears instead of peaches or mangoes.
This salad makes an ideal finish to a summer Christmas lunch or dinner.

SERVES 4

juice of 2 oranges

juice of ½ lemon

1 tablespoon castor sugar

200 g (7 oz) punnet raspberries

3 peaches

1 medium mango

8 large strawberries

2 small pawpaws

Blend the orange and lemon juices, sugar and two-thirds of the raspberries to a purée. Strain into a serving bowl.

Wash the peaches and cut each into 8–12 segments. Peel the mango and cut into small pieces. Wash and slice the strawberries. Add all the fruits to the bowl with remaining whole raspberries. Stir gently and refrigerate.

Remove the salad from the refrigerator about 15 minutes before required. Just before serving, halve and peel the pawpaws and, with a spoon, scoop out the seeds. Spoon the fruit salad into the pawpaws and serve.

Baked rhubarb & apple with grapefruit

This dessert is delicious hot or cold. To present it attractively, I sometimes use a piece of PVC pipe of 10 cm (4 in) in diameter and 5 cm (2 in) high. You can also use a round pastry cutter about 10 cm (4 in) in diameter, or just serve the fruits in individual soufflé bowls.

SERVES 2

2 Golden Delicious apples, peeled, halved, cored and cut into eighths

4 stalks rhubarb, peeled and cut into 4 cm (1¾ in) pieces

2 tablespoons castor sugar

3 tablespoons water

2 grapefruit

Preheat the oven to 180°C/350°F/Gas Mark 4.

In a bowl, gently toss together the apple, rhubarb and sugar. Place in a roasting tray with the water and bake in a preheated oven until just soft. This takes 15–20 minutes.

Peel the grapefruit, taking care to remove all the pith. Cut the grapefruit into segments, collecting any juice that results. To cut segments, use a small, sharp knife and insert the blade into the grapefruit along the fine skin which separates the sections. Turn the blade and come up the other side of the skin to release the fruit segment from its casing.

Place the PVC ring or pastry cutter on the plate. Spoon half the apple and rhubarb into the ring and top with grapefruit segments. Spoon over the cooking juices from the rhubarb and apple, and any grapefruit juice. Carefully lift off the ring before serving.

Stewed figs & plums in Red wine

Here is a luscious autumn weekend dessert. The dish is lovely either hot
or cold but I prefer it cold as the spices have released more of their flavour.

SERVES 4–6

½ bottle (375 ml) good red wine

125 ml (4 fl oz) water

4 tablespoons castor sugar

¼ vanilla pod, cut open lengthwise

2 cm (1 in) piece cinnamon stick

½ star anise

6 just-ripe blood plums, left whole

8 just-ripe black figs, left whole

Place the red wine, water, sugar, vanilla pod,
cinnamon and star anise in a medium saucepan.
Bring to the boil and simmer for 10 minutes.

Add the washed plums and figs to the pan, return
to a simmer and cook for about 10 minutes.

Gently place the fruit in a bowl and pour over the
liquid. If you wish the juice to have a stronger flavour,
boil it to reduce the juice by half before pouring over
the fruits.

Allow to cool before serving. If not using immediately,
refrigerate and remove from the refrigerator
20 minutes before serving.

Caramelized red plums with berries

This is a truly luscious dish with a magnificent ruby-red colour.
For presentation, sprinkle icing sugar on top just before serving.

SERVES 6

½ vanilla pod

5 tablespoons castor sugar

200 g (7 oz) punnet raspberries

200 g (7 oz) punnet blueberries

juice of 1 orange

juice of ½ lemon

6–12 red plums, halved and stoned

200 g (7 oz) punnet blackberries

a little icing sugar from a shaker

Split the vanilla pod in half and, using the blade of a small knife, scrape out the tiny black seeds. Mix these seeds with the sugar.

In a food processor blend half of the raspberries, one-third of the blueberries, the orange juice, lemon juice and half of the vanilla sugar to a purée. Strain this berry sauce into a jug.

Sprinkle the remaining sugar over the cut plums and place under a hot grill until the sugar starts to bubble.

Pour a little berry sauce into the centre of each plate. Place 2–4 plum halves on the sauce and arrange the blackberries and the remaining fruits around. Sprinkle with a little icing sugar and serve.

Pear & Prune loaf

There is no added sugar or fat in this fruity loaf – the sweetness
and moisture of the dried fruits are enough.
You will need a 20 cm (8 in) greased loaf tin or, if you wish, a round or square tin.

MAKES ABOUT 12 SLICES

10 dried pear halves

10 dried apricots

20 dried prunes

4 dried apple rings, halved

500 ml (18 fl oz) water

1 large banana

115 g (4 oz) wholemeal self-raising flour

55 g (2 oz) ground almonds

¼ teaspoon cinnamon powder

1 teaspoon finely grated orange rind

Place the pears, apricots, prunes and apple rings in a saucepan with the water. Bring to the boil, cover and simmer for 5 minutes. Remove the apricots and apple rings from the pan and blend them to a purée with the cooking liquid and the banana. Place this purée in a large mixing bowl.

Preheat the oven to 180°C/350°F/Gas Mark 4.

Mix the flour and ground almonds with the fruit purée and gently stir in the cinnamon powder and orange rind. Spoon about a quarter of this into the cake tin. Top with half of the dried pear halves and then layer with another quarter of the cake preparation. Add a layer of prunes (use them all), and another quarter of the cake preparation. Lastly, add the remaining pears and top with the remaining cake preparation. Tap the tin to remove any air and bake in the preheated oven for 40 minutes. Allow to cool before unmoulding onto a rack.

Cool and store in an airtight container. This loaf keeps for 2–3 days.

French-style pancakes

French pancakes are called crêpes and are a very popular family dessert.
Serve them with freshly sliced fruits or with lemon and sugar.
You need a crêpe pan or a small non-stick frying pan about 18 cm (about 7 in) in diameter.

MAKES 6–8 CRÊPES

115 g (4 oz) plain flour, sifted

a pinch of salt

1 teaspoon castor sugar

1 egg

about 250 ml (9 fl oz) milk

1 teaspoon groundnut oil

1 teaspoon butter

4 lemon wedges

Place the flour, salt and sugar in a mixing bowl. Make a well in the centre and pour in the egg and half of the milk. Using a whisk, first mix the egg and milk together, then gradually incorporate the flour, slowly adding the rest of the milk to form a smooth, thin mixture.

Strain the preparation through a fine strainer and refrigerate for at least 20 minutes or until required. If you are in a great rush, you can use it immediately, but the crêpes will not be as smooth.

Heat the oil and butter in a small non-stick pan or crêpe pan until it turns a light golden colour. Whisk this melted butter into the crêpe batter. Return the pan to a high heat and when it is hot, pour in enough mixture to coat the bottom of the pan. Twirl the pan in a smooth motion to form a thin, even crêpe. When the upper half of the crêpe starts to become dry and the lower half is golden brown, pick up the crêpe with a spatula and turn it quickly to cook the other side. After browning the second side, remove the crêpe and place it on a plate.

Without adding any more butter or oil to the pan, make the rest of the crêpes in the same way. If a crêpe begins to stick, wipe the pan with absorbent paper, melt a little butter in the pan and proceed.

Serve with wedges of lemon.

Pear Pudding

Enjoy this easy-to-prepare pudding either on its own or with the Sweet Creamy Topping on p. 182. You will need 4 individual buttered soufflé moulds and 4 pieces of foil to cover them.

SERVES 4

400 g (14 oz) can of pear
  halves in natural juice

1 large egg

1 tablespoon brown sugar

115 g (4 oz) wholemeal self-raising flour

1 tablespoon melted butter
  (or margarine if you must)

1 tablespoon honey

1 tablespoon sultanas

Preheat the oven to 200°C/400°F/Gas Mark 6.

Drain the pear halves, reserving the juice. Dice the pears.

In a medium bowl beat the egg and sugar for 2 minutes. Stir in the flour and pear juice alternately, half at a time. Lastly, stir in the melted butter and diced pears.

Spoon a quarter of the honey into each buttered soufflé mould. Sprinkle a quarter of the sultanas into each mould, then spoon the pudding preparation into moulds. Tap the moulds gently to get rid of any air bubbles and cover with foil. Place the moulds in a roasting tray. Add boiling water from the kettle to the tray to a level of 2 cm (3/4 in) up the sides of the moulds. Carefully place the tray in the preheated oven and cook for 30 minutes.

Remove from the oven and peel back the foil. Run a thin blade around the edge of the moulds, turn out the puddings onto plates and serve.

Rice pudding & glacé pineapple & apricots

This is a satisfying family dessert. If you wish, replace the pineapple and apricot with other glacé fruits. Dried fruits work as well—just soak the fruits in warm water for about 1 hour before using.

SERVES ABOUT 6

175 g (6 oz) short-grain rice

1 litre (1¾ pints) milk

4 tablespoons castor sugar

1 teaspoon grated orange zest

4 rings glacé pineapple, diced

4 pieces glacé apricots, diced

55 g (2 oz) pistachio nuts, finely chopped

Place the rice in a saucepan with a large quantity of cold water. Bring to the boil and boil for 4 minutes. Drain.

Bring the milk to the boil in a large saucepan. Add the rice, cover and simmer very gently for about 30 minutes, after which time the mixture should be creamy. Pay attention to the last few minutes of the cooking to ensure that the rice does not stick or burn.

Add the sugar, orange zest and glacé fruits. Stir well and cook for a further 2–3 minutes. Pour into a deep serving dish, sprinkle over the pistachio nuts and serve either hot or cold.

Baked nectarines with Raspberries

In this easy, special-occasion dessert you can use peaches or red
plums instead of nectarines. Cook it in a large gratin or porcelain quiche dish.
It is also quite attractive cooked and served in individual dishes.

SERVES 4

¼ vanilla pod

2 tablespoons castor sugar

about 16 raspberries

4 ripe nectarines, cut into eighths

3 tablespoons water

½ teaspoon rose water (optional)

a few chopped pistachio nuts *or*
   1 tablespoon toasted, flaked
   almonds (optional)

Preheat the oven to 220°C (450°F).

Halve the vanilla pod lengthwise and use your fingertips
to rub the sugar against the black seeds inside the pod.
This flavours the sugar.

Mash the raspberries with a third of the sugar and place
in a gratin dish. Arrange the nectarines on top,
overlapping the segments as you go. Sprinkle over the
water and rose water, and sprinkle with the remaining
castor sugar.

Bake in a preheated oven for about 20 minutes or until
the nectarines are soft and the edges lightly browned.
Sprinkle the pistachios or almonds on top and serve hot
or cold.

Apple tart on filo

Apple tart is the most popular dessert in bistros in France.
This is a very light version that uses filo pastry instead of the
traditional puff or shortcrust pastry.

SERVES 4

6 Granny Smith apples

3 tablespoons water

4 sheets filo pastry

a little groundnut *or* walnut oil

1 tablespoon cream, low-fat
  if you wish (optional)

1 tablespoon castor sugar

3 tablespoons apricot jam
  or a little icing sugar

Peel, quarter and core two of the apples. Cook them
with the water in a covered pan until soft. Mash the
apple and allow to cool.

Peel, halve and core the remaining four apples, then
cut them into 2 mm ($^1/_{10}$ in) slices.

Line a baking sheet with baking paper. Top with one
sheet of filo pastry. Brush the pastry with a little oil and
place a second sheet of pastry on top. Do likewise
with the third and fourth sheets of pastry, brushing
each sheet with oil as you go. Cut four rounds of
pastry by placing a saucer on top of the pastry sheet
and going around the edge of the saucer with the
blade of a knife. Discard leftover pastry.

Preheat the oven to 200°C/400°F/Gas Mark 6.

Stir cream into the cold apple purée and spread the
purée over the pastry rounds. Place the apple slices on
top of the purée, overlapping slightly so there are no
gaps. You will probably have some left over – be as
creative as you like with the pattern of the apple slices.

Sprinkle the top with castor sugar and cook in a hot
oven for 15 minutes. The pastry should be crisp and
the edges of the apple slightly browned. Before
serving, brush the tops of the tarts with warm apricot
jam or dust with icing sugar.

BASICS

In this final section I have given recipes for stocks and sauces that you will find very useful. Stocks are used to make tasty soups, casseroles and sauces, and a home-made stock tastes so much better and is far healthier than commercial ones. If you are using commercial stocks, read the list of ingredients carefully before buying as some contain monosodium glutamate (MSG) or are very salty. The 'star' sauce in this book is the Italian-style tomato sauce that I use in various recipes. It is full of natural flavour, is low in fat and is easy to learn to make. It can be adapted by adding herbs, spices and vegetables. The other sauces are particularly useful to those who love sauces and are on a low-fat diet.

Vegetable stock

This stock is especially handy for vegetarians to use instead of a chicken or veal stock. Cover and store in the refrigerator for 2 to 3 days or for up to one month in the freezer.

MAKES ABOUT 2 LITRES (4 ½ PINTS)

2 teaspoons olive oil

1 onion, sliced

2 carrots, sliced

2 sticks celery, sliced

2 mushrooms, sliced (optional)

1 small leek, sliced

about 3 litres (5¼ pints) cold water

1 sprig of thyme

a few sprigs of parsley

½ clove

salt and freshly ground
    black pepper

Heat the oil in a non-stick pan and stir-fry the onion until lightly browned. Add the carrot, celery, mushrooms and leek and stir-fry for another 2 minutes before adding the water, thyme, parsley and clove. Season and simmer, uncovered, for 25 minutes.

Strain the stock and allow to cool before storing.

Chicken stock

A chicken stock is such a useful preparation for flavouring soups, sauces and stews. When your stock is made you can boil it down to a smaller quantity, cool and store in the refrigerator for 3–4 days or frozen for up to a month.

MAKES ABOUT 2 LITRES (4½ PINTS)

approx. 1 kg (about 2 lb 4 oz) chicken bones (carcass, neck, wings – skin and fat removed)

3 litres (5¼ pints) water

1 carrot, sliced

1 onion, sliced

1 stick celery or a piece of leek, sliced

a small pinch of salt

5 black peppercorns, crushed

1 clove

a few sprigs of parsley

a small sprig of thyme

½ bay leaf

Place the chicken bones and water in a large saucepan. Bring to the boil and skim with a spoon to remove any scum that floats to the surface. Add the carrot, onion, celery, salt, peppercorns, clove and herbs and simmer for about 1 hour, skimming the surface again if necessary. Strain the stock and discard the bones and vegetables. Allow to cool, remove any fat that forms at the surface and store.

Beef or veal stock

A stock is like an infusion, the idea being to obtain meat flavour from the bones. If beef bones are not available, use veal, lamb or pork bones together with some beef and veal trimmings. This preparation takes about 3 hours, so plan ahead. Alternatively, use a commercial veal or beef stock.

MAKES 1 LITRE (2 PINTS)

1 kg (2lb 2 oz) beef and veal trimmings

2 kg (4 lb 4 oz) veal bones

1 large onion, quartered

2 carrots, cut into bite-size pieces

1 tablespoon groundnut oil

2 sticks celery, cut into bite-size pieces

1 clove

6 peppercorns, crushed

a few sprigs of parsley

1 bay leaf

2 sprigs of thyme

a pinch of salt

Place the meat trimmings into a large saucepan with plenty of water and leave to stand for an hour or so. Preheat the oven to 240°C/475°F/Gas Mark 9).

Place the bones, onion and carrots in a roasting tray and toss with the oil to coat. Place in the preheated oven and cook for 15–25 minutes to brown the bones and vegetables (avoid burning the vegetables). Remove from the oven and add to the meat trimmings in the saucepan, taking care to discard all the fat. Add the chopped celery, clove, peppercorns, parsley, bay leaf, thyme and salt. Bring to a simmer, skimming the surface from time to time with a mesh spoon to remove the scum.

After 3 hours, strain the stock into a saucepan and boil to reduce to about 1 litre (2 pints). Cool the stock, skim off any fat that rises to the surface and refrigerate or freeze. The stock keeps in the fridge for 3–4 days or up to 1 month in the freezer.

Fish stock

Made with fresh, cleaned fish bones, this flavoursome
liquid is handy to have for steaming or poaching fish fillets.
It is also used in the preparation of fish soups and sauces.

MAKES ABOUT 1 LITRE (1 ¾ PINTS)

500 g (about 1 lb) fresh fish bones such
as cod or haddock, but no freshwater
fish or salmon

1 teaspoon groundnut oil

1 small carrot, peeled and finely sliced

1 medium onion, peeled and finely sliced

1 stick celery, finely sliced

10 cm (4 in) piece of leek, finely sliced

a few sprigs of parsley

1 sprig of thyme

½ bay leaf

250 ml (9 fl oz) dry white wine

1½ litres (about 2¾ pints) water

salt and freshly ground black pepper

Wash the fish bones in water and remove any blood or
dark skin.

In a large non-stick saucepan, heat the oil and stir-fry
the vegetables for 5 minutes without browning. Add
the herbs, fish bones, wine and water. Season with a
little salt and pepper, bring to the boil and simmer for
20 minutes.

Strain the stock, pressing gently on the bones and
vegetables to extract the flavour. Return the stock to
the pan, bring to the boil and reduce to approximately
1 litre (1¾ pints) or less. The stock may be stored in a
covered container in the refrigerator for 2–3 days or
frozen for up to a month.

Peanut sauce

This sauce is the richest one in the book, and I recommend using it in moderation.
It is a good accompaniment to steamed vegetables, rice, noodles and kebabs.

SERVES 4

2 cm (1 in) piece of ginger

1/2 small onion

1 clove garlic

175 ml (6 fl oz) water

4 tablespoons desiccated coconut

1 teaspoon groundnut oil

1/2 teaspoon curry powder

2 teaspoons fish sauce *or* soy sauce

2 tablespoons crunchy peanut butter

1/2 teaspoon chilli paste

Blend the ginger, onion and garlic to a purée or, if you prefer, chop them finely.

Place the water in a saucepan with the coconut and bring to the boil for 10 seconds. Turn off the heat and allow the coconut to infuse.

In a small non-stick saucepan on low heat, gently fry the onion purée in oil for 5 minutes, stirring with a wooden spoon to prevent burning. Add the curry powder and fish sauce and stir well before adding the peanut butter and chilli paste.

Strain the coconut liquid into a bowl, pressing on the coconut to extract as much flavour as possible. Add the liquid to the peanut sauce and stir until the sauce is smooth. Cook on low heat for 2 minutes. It is now ready to serve.

Pesto

Pesto is more of a seasoning than a sauce. Its main ingredient is the very aromatic herb, basil, and 1 teaspoon of it is sufficient to season steamed vegetables or a portion of grilled fish or meat. Pesto is most commonly used with pasta. Store your pesto in a sealed jar in the refrigerator, and after each use, add a little olive oil to the jar to seal the pesto and prevent it from going off. Pesto keeps for up to two weeks in the fridge.

MAKES ABOUT 250 ML (9 FL OZ)

1 cup very fresh unblemished
  basil leaves

3 tablespoons pinenuts

3 cloves garlic, peeled

3 tablespoons grated parmesan

3 tablespoons olive oil

Discard any blemished basil leaves. Wash the leaves, drain well and dry with a clean tea towel.

In a food processor, place the basil, pinenuts, garlic and parmesan. Blend to a paste. Slowly drizzle in the oil and blend until the mixture is well combined.

If not using immediately, cover with a film of olive oil and store in a sealed jar in the refrigerator.

Italian-style tomato sauce

The soft, sweet, rich texture of tomatoes makes them extremely versatile. This Italian-style tomato sauce can be used with pasta, fish, vegetables, meat, pancakes and pizzas. You can add your own personal touch at the end by adding a herb or spice of your choice, such as basil, tarragon, cumin or chilli. If you wish, double the quantities and freeze what is not required.

MAKES ABOUT 600 ML (1 PINT)

about 1 kg (about 2 lb 4 oz) medium-ripe tomatoes, cut into eighths

½ medium onion, peeled and diced

1 stick celery, from the heart, diced

1 medium carrot, peeled and diced

2 sprigs of parsley

1 sprig of thyme

1 clove garlic, crushed

1 teaspoon tomato pureé

freshly ground black pepper

1 teaspoon olive oil (optional)

Place the tomatoes and other vegetables in a saucepan with the herbs, garlic, tomato paste and a little pepper. Cook, uncovered, on medium heat for 20 minutes.

Remove the herbs and pass the vegetables through a food mill or fine strainer. Check for seasoning and season if you wish. Stir in the oil before serving the sauce. It is best served warm.

chef's note

For the sauce a food mill gives the best results as it does not allow the tomato skins to go through. If you use a food processor or blender, pass the sauce through a fine strainer.

Curry & tomato sauce

Serve this sauce with steamed vegetables and rice. It is also good with grilled fish or meat.

SERVES ABOUT 4

½ onion

2 cm (1 in) piece of ginger

2 cloves garlic

2 teaspoons groundnut oil

4 fennel seeds

10 cumin seeds

2 teaspoons curry powder

6 large tomatoes, seeded and finely chopped

3 tablespoons cooked lentils, from a can

125 ml (4 fl oz) hot water

¼ teaspoon chilli paste (optional)

1 tablespoon desiccated coconut or 1 tablespoon finely sliced coriander leaves (optional)

Peel the onion, ginger and garlic, then blend them together to a fine purée. Alternatively, chop finely.

In a medium non-stick saucepan place the oil, fennel seeds, cumin seeds and puréed onion, ginger and garlic. Cook on low heat for at least 5 minutes while stirring with a wooden spoon. If the ingredients start to burn add a tablespoon or two of water. Add the curry powder and stir for about 1 minute before adding the tomato and lentils. Bring to a simmer, add the hot water and cook on low heat for about 10 minutes, stirring occasionally.

Just before serving, stir in the chilli paste and desiccated coconut or coriander leaves if desired.

Many vegetables
can be cooked in
stock, blended into
a purée, and
served as a sauce
with fish, meat or
other vegetables.

Red pepper Sauce

The smooth texture of cooked red pepper makes a delicious, strongly flavoured sauce that is perfect for pasta, grilled fish or grilled vegetables.

MAKES ABOUT 500 ML (1 PINT)

2 large red peppers

1 ½ tablespoons olive oil

½ onion, chopped

2 large tomatoes, cut into eighths

1 stick celery, diced

1 clove garlic, chopped

1 sprig of thyme

a few sprigs of parsley

salt and freshly ground black pepper

Halve the pepper, remove the seeds and cut each half into about 8 pieces.

Heat 1 tablespoon of oil in a non-stick pan and on low heat stir-fry the onion and pepper for about 5 minutes.

Add the tomatoes, celery, garlic, thyme and parsley to the pepper and season with a little salt and pepper. Cover and simmer for about 20 minutes. Remove the thyme and parsley and pass the sauce through a food mill, or blend to a purée and pass through a fine strainer. Check for seasoning and stir in the remaining oil before serving. If the sauce is too thick, dilute with some boiling water from the kettle.

Chilli dipping sauce

This spicy sauce is delicious with steamed vegetables, samosas and food served in filo pastry. Consume it in moderation as it is fairly salty, sweet and spicy.

SERVES 4

3 tablespoons water

1 tablespoon sugar

2 teaspoons white-wine vinegar

1 tablespoon fish sauce

½ clove garlic, finely chopped

¼ teaspoon hot chilli paste (sambal oelek)

1 tablespoon roasted peanuts, chopped

In a saucepan bring the water and sugar to a simmer and boil for 2 minutes. Allow to cool.

Mix in the vinegar, fish sauce, garlic, chilli paste and peanuts and serve.

Spicy pea & carrot sauce

This lovely sauce is very low in fat and full of goodness.
Serve it with grilled, steamed or pan-fried meat or fish, or with vegetables.

SERVES 4–6

1 teaspoon groundnut oil

¼ onion, finely chopped

¼ teaspoon curry powder

1 large tomato, diced

1 medium carrot, finely sliced

375 ml (13 fl oz) chicken (p. 204) *or* vegetable stock (p. 203)

55 g (2 oz) shelled peas

a pinch of chilli pepper

salt and freshly ground black pepper

Heat the oil in a non-stick saucepan and fry the onion and curry powder for 3 minutes. Add the tomato and stir well. Add the carrot and chicken stock, and bring to the boil. Add the peas and season with chilli pepper and a little salt and pepper. Cook for about 15 minutes until the vegetables are tender.

Blend the vegetables and liquid to a smooth sauce and strain if you wish. If the sauce is too thick, dilute with a little hot water from the kettle.

Menus for Special Occasions

Mother's Day

Broccoli Soup with a Hint of Curry (p. 44)

Pan-fried Salmon with Dill and Vegetables (p. 127)

Pear Pudding (p. 195)

Father's Day

Chicken in Red-Wine Sauce with Carrots (p. 151)

Green Salad with Walnut Dressing (p. 56)

Apple Tart on Filo (p. 198)

Christmas Day

Smoked Salmon and Avocado Parcels (p. 79)

Roast Christmas Turkey with Bread and Orange Stuffing (p. 154–55)

Green Salad with Walnut Dressing (p. 56)

Your Favourite Christmas Pudding *or* Peach, Mango and Berry Salad in Pawpaw (p. 187)

A Romantic Dinner

Asparagus Soup (p. 44)

Salmon Tartlets on Filo (p. 137)

Williams Pears and Passionfruit Salad (p. 183)

A Fish Dinner

Scallops, Asparagus and Salad (p. 141)

Fish and Prawn Soup with Fennel (p. 49)

Fresh Mango

A Vegetarian Dinner

Cauliflower and Mushroom Curry (p. 118)

Tomato and Spicy Bean Tartlets on Filo (p. 93)

Fresh Fruit Platter with Two Berry Sauces (p. 184)

A Light Alfresco Lunch

Salade Niçoise (p. 61)

Peach, Mango and Berry Fruit Salad in Pawpaw (p. 187)

An Italian Meal

Focaccia with Olives and Thyme (p. 72)

Risotto with Chicken and Vegetables (p. 108)

Seasonal Fruits with Fresh Ricotta Cheese

A Chinese Meal

Stir-fried Vegetables with Roast Pork (p. 176)

Spicy Stir-fried Prawns with Bok Choy (p. 138)

Seasonal Fruits

An Indian Meal

Vegetable Samosas (p. 76)

Curried Mackerel with Coriander and Celery (p. 136)

Dates and Orange on Yoghurt (p. 182)

A French Meal

Artichokes Provençale (p. 120)

Grilled Loin of Lamb Provençale (p. 170)

Fresh Berries

One-dish Dinners

Serve any of these with a salad.

Minestrone Soup (p. 47)

Vegetarian Pizza (p. 88)

Couscous with Grilled Lamb Kebabs (p. 175)

Tagliatelle Marinara with Vegetables (p. 132)

Paella (p. 109)

Singapore-style Noodles (p. 105)

Risotto with Chicken and Vegetables (p. 108)

CONVERSION CHARTS

Symbols used in this book

ml = millilitre

mm = millimetre

cm = centimetre

L = litre

oz = ounce

lb = pound

in = inches

Volume Measurements (workable approximates)

Spoon measurements refer to British Standard measuring spoons.

5 ml = 1 teaspoon

15 ml = 1 tablespoon

60 ml = 2 fl oz

125 ml = 4½ fl oz

150 ml = ¼ pint

250 ml = 9 fl oz

275 ml = ½ pint

375 ml = 13 fl oz

500 ml = 18 fl oz

Measures (workable approximates)

1 cm =   ⅓ in

2 cm =   ¾ in

2.5 cm =   1 in

5 cm =   2 in

10 cm = 4 in

20 cm = 8 in

Weight Measurements (workable approximates)

15 g = ½ oz

30 g = 1 oz

55 g = 2 oz

100 g = 3½ oz

115 g = 4 oz

150 g = 5½ oz

175 g = 6 oz

200 g = 7 oz

225 g = 8 oz

250 g = 9 oz

300 g = 11 oz

350 g = 12 oz

400 g = 14 oz

450 g = 1 lb

500 g = 1 lb 2 oz

1 kg = 2 lb 4 oz

Oven Temperatures (workable approximates)

110°C = 225°F	Very low	Gas Mark ¼
120°C = 250°F	Very low	Gas Mark ½
140°C = 275°F	Low	Gas Mark 1
150°C = 300°F	Low	Gas Mark 2
160°C = 325°F	Moderate	Gas Mark 3
180°C = 350°F	Moderate	Gas Mark 4
190°C = 375°F	Moderately hot	Gas Mark 5
200°C = 400°F	Moderately hot	Gas Mark 6
220°C = 425°F	Hot	Gas Mark 7
230°C = 450°F	Hot	Gas Mark 8
240°C = 475°F	Very hot	Gas Mark 9

GLOSSARY

abalone mushroom   see mushroom

al dente   An Italian expression, meaning 'to the tooth', usually used in reference to the cooking of pasta to a degree that offers a little resistance when bitten into, but is not soft.

baste (to)   To spoon or brush food, usually roasts, with liquid or fat to keep the meat moist.

bean sprouts   The sprout of the mung bean, very popular in Asian cooking. It is usually sold by weight or packets in markets and foodstores.

blanch (to)   To plunge food for a brief time into boiling water in order to precook or soften it.

bok choy   A very popular variety of small Chinese cabbage. It is usually sold in bunches of three heads. Available from many greengrocers and most Asian foodstores.

Chinese broccoli   A green leafy Chinese vegetable used extensively in Asian cuisine, especially in stir-fries and soups. Both the stems and leaves of the vegetable can be eaten.

Chinese cabbage   Also known as *wong nga bak*. There are many varieties available, and the one most commonly used looks like an elongated cabbage. They have pale yellow to pale green tightly bunched leaves.

chop (to)   To cut ingredients into tiny pieces. Herbs are best chopped using a 20 cm (8 in) or longer chef's knife. For casserole dishes such as a curry, you can use a food processor to chop up ingredients such as onion and ginger.

coriander   Also known as cilantro, especially in the US. This is a herb with small leaves and a strong, pungent flavour. The leaves are used in Asian and Middle-Eastern cooking, and the roots are used as part of a spice mixture in Thai curries. Available from most greengrocers.

couscous   A form of pasta made from coarse wheat semolina. Available from most supermarkets and gourmet food stores and usually comes in 500 g (1 lb 2 oz) packs. Couscous is a staple food in North African countries and is served with vegetables, fish and meat.

dice (to)   To cut food into 1 cm (⅓ in) cubes, especially vegetables. To dice, the food is first sliced, then cut into small sticks (batons) and finally cut across into small squares.

dried bean-curd   A by-product of the soybean, and popular in Asian vegetarian cooking. Available in the refrigerated section at Asian foodstores. It comes in air-tight plastic packs of 4 or 6 squares.

egg noodles   These come in many varieties – thin, thick, fresh or dried. The recipes in the book usually call for Hokkien noodles or egg noodles, and they are readily available from the refrigerated section of Chinese grocers. Reconstitute dried noodles in boiling water for about 3 minutes or until they are soft, then proceed with the recipe.

filo pastry   A very thin Greek pastry that is relatively low in fat and easy to use for wrapping around foods. Available from Greek gourmet foodstores and in the refrigerated section of most supermarkets.

fish sauce   A salty, strong-flavoured Asian sauce popular in Thai and Vietnamese cooking. It is made from fish extract and used as a seasoning. The salt content varies from brand to brand, so use it in moderation and taste the dish as you are cooking.

flageolet beans   A variety of small French kidney beans that are pale green to creamy white in colour. They can be purchased dried or canned from good supermarkets.

focaccia   A flat Italian bread available from Italian gourmet shops and some bakers. A recipe for focaccia is provided on page 72.

glacé fruit   Also called candied fruit. Fruit preserved in a sugar syrup; usually used in desserts.

glaze (to)   To brush pastry or finished desserts with jam, fat, milk or egg yolk to give a shiny finish.

grill (to)   Refers to either cooking under an oven grill or on a grill on top of the stove or barbecue. Top-of-the-stove grills are usually made of cast-iron.

harissa   A hot chilli paste made from dried chillies, garlic, cumin and other spices. It is popular in North African countries where it is used to flavour soups, stews and casseroles, and couscous. Available in jars from gourmet foodstores and supermarkets. Substitute with an Asian-style chilli paste or sambal oelek.

marinate (to)   To coat or cover meat, fish or poultry with a seasoning of liquids, spices and herbs.

mushroom, abalone   A medium-sized mushroom with a subtle flavour, popular in Chinese cuisine. Available fresh from some greengrocers.

mushroom, cloud ear   Also called *wun yee* or wood ear mushroom. A Chinese mushroom, sold dried in Chinese grocers. When dry, it is black and curly and looks like seaweed. To use, soak in hot water until the mushroom is soft and has increased in size. It has a crunchy, bland flavour.

oyster sauce   A salty, strongly flavoured Asian sauce made from an extract of oysters. If possible, select a brand without monosodium glutamate.

poach (to)   To gently cook food, covered, in a hot or simmering liquid.

polenta   A coarse cornmeal popular in Italy. It is cooked in water until it forms a paste and then baked or pan-fried and served with meat, fish or vegetables. A recipe is provided on page 90.

ratatouille   A dish of mixed cooked vegetables, including tomato, aubergine, pepper, courgettes, olive oil and herbs. Popular in the south of France.

reduce (to)   To diminish the quantity of a liquid or sauce by boiling it in order to obtain a smaller quantity, greater concentration of flavour and thicker consistency.

refresh (to)   To cool food by holding it under cold running water. Usually for the purpose of arresting the cooking process.

rice, Arborio A short-grain Italian rice used for risotto. Available from good supermarkets and Italian foodstores.

rice, basmati An aromatic long-grain rice that releases a floral smell during cooking and a fine texture. Usually served with curries and Indian food.

sambal oelek A hot chilli paste used in Asian cooking. Available in jars from supermarkets and Asian foodstores.

sesame oil A very flavoursome oil made from sesame seeds. It can be overpowering, so use it in small quantities.

shaoshing wine A Chinese wine made from rice and used in small quantities in Asian cooking for flavouring. It has an alcohol content of 16 per cent. Available from Chinese foodstores and keeps well for months in the pantry.

simmer (to) To cook food in a liquid that is just below boiling point, when the bubbles are just about to break on the surface.

small sticks Usually referring to the way vegetables are cut. The vegetable, for example, a carrot, is first cut into 5 or 6 cm (about 2 in) lengths, which are then sliced lengthwise (approx. 5 mm thick ($1/5$ in) and then cut lengthwise again into 5 mm ($1/5$ in) sticks.

soy sauce There are many varieties of soy sauce and some are saltier than others. Made from an extract of soybeans, wheat flour and other seasonings.

steam (to) Usually refers to the cooking of food in a steamer but can also refer to cooking by steam in a small amount of liquid in a covered saucepan.

stir-fry (to) To cook food in a little oil while stirring and tossing to stop the food from sticking or burning. When stir-frying vegetables it is sometimes necessary to add a little water down the side of the wok or pan to stop the vegetables from burning.

tahini A flavoursome paste made from sesame seeds and used as a spread. It is an ingredient of hummus, the Middle-Eastern dip made with chickpeas.

tamarind A small, tropical, acidic fruit shaped like a broad bean. It is available as a paste or dried from Asian foodstores. When using the dried form, soak a small piece in some hot water. Drain after 10 minutes and strain off the juice. Use the juice and discard the solids.

wun yee see mushroom, cloud ear

INdex

Numerals in **bold** indicate colour plates.